Education

Education
Back to the Future

Len Solo

Education: Back to the Future

Copyright © 2014 Len Solo and the
Alternative Education Resource Organization (AERO)

All rights reserved.

No part of this book may be reproduced or reprinted in any form without written permission from Len Solo and the Alternative Education Resource Organization.

Alternative Education Resource Organization
417 Roslyn Road
Roslyn Heights, NY 11577

Cover: Black Dog Design, kim@blackdogdesign.com
Layout: Isaac Graves
Editorial Assistance: Jessica Graves

Photo Credits: p. 105 and back cover (right and bottom)—Photos courtesy of the author; Back cover (top)—Photo by and courtesy of Mary DiSchino.

Illustrations: p. x—Drawing originally found in The Teacher Paper (Portland, OR, est. 1975), but original artist and author of new captions is unknown; p. 1—Lenny Solo; pp. 7, 71, and 83—Artists unknown; pp. 14, 33, & 47—Drawings by Steven Kling; p. 57—Phillip (last name unknown).

Printed in the United States of America.

Library of Congress Control Number: 2014940603
ISBN: 978-0974525280

The "Introduction" was initially published as "The Second Coming, Sort Of," AERO-Gramme #22, Fall 1997; then, revised, in *Turning Points: 35 Visionaries in Education Tell Their Stories*, edited by Jerry Mintz and Carlo Ricci (Alternative Education Resources Organization, pp. 360-368 (2010). All other chapters, except the conclusion, were initially published in small educational journals and all have been extensively revised.

How odd it is that anyone should
not see that all observations must
be for or against some views, if they
are to be of any service.
—Charles Darwin

Contents

vii   Foreword by Herbert Kohl
xi   Introduction

1   He Often Creates Out of His Fullness

7   Oh, Wow, Dad-dy, I Know My Alphabets

15   Beard With Holes

33   Strawberry Fields Forever?

47   New School Curriculum Report

57   One of You Is Sufficient

71   Community and Education

83   Conclusions: Backward and Forward

Foreword

In these days, when the commodification and quantification of childhood dominate the language of educational "reform," when the arts, literature, politics, cultural studies, and poetry are casually eliminated from children's learning, and the cancelation of a kindergarten theater production is justified because it takes away from test prep time and supposedly threatens future job possibilities for five-year-olds, Len Solo's accumulated wisdom of half a century working in the service of children and the communities they live in is most welcome. The tales and anecdotes in this book are refreshing—they remind me of all the wonderful times I have had teaching and being a parent—of love for children because of who they are and what they might become, not because they can be given a positive dollar value or improve someone's test numbers.

Like Len Solo, I have been fighting for young people and for social justice for over 50 years, and this book r eminds me of how important the fight for decent communities and convivial childhood continues to be. Len's stories and reflections begin with his work in the 1960s at the Teacher Drop-Out Center through his work as principal of the Graham & Parks Alternative Public School in Cambridge, Massachusetts, and up to the present.

I remember encountering some of the stories in this book over the years. One, about teaching a unit about blueberries and other food products has stuck with me. The usual way to approach such a topic in the classroom is through studying how and where they grow, what their nutritional value is, and how to integrate them into your diet. Len points out that there are some things missing here: who produces the food, what are the lives of such people like, who can afford to buy the products, who benefits from the sales: in other words, what is the social and economic background of the, often poor, working people who usually remain invisible in the curriculum. And how is profit made from their labor distributed. Teaching about blueberries can and should be dangerous.

One of central ideas in the book is to develop the classroom and the school as a community. For Len Solo, the end product of learning is social activism. Len's work has always integrated class, equity, and culture into the mix of what is studied. His work is education on the side of justice. It is focused on the most neglected aspect of current debates on school reform these days, the child and her or his best ways of learning. Placing that at the center of his narrative, Solo moves out to consider the place parents, educators, and other forces within the community and larger society play in the development of a future worthy of our children.

This personal overview of the range of public and private alternative schools from the 1960s through the present is a reminder of how much has been done and undone in the struggle to achieve equity and justice in education and life for all children. It is a wonderful tour through fifty years of educational struggle which should inspire those of us who were there and inform and motivate young educators who place themselves on the side of children and dare to pursue a career teaching for justice, equity, and for the fun and joy of learning at a time when corporate interests, academic statisticians, and arrogant politicians feel comfortable with manipulating childhood for their sense of what corporate society demands rather than what people care to do. The book comes down solidly on the side of conviviality, of the quest for a decent community in which, as a graffiti painted on a wall in Chile during Allende's time proclaimed: "In the future, the only privileged ones will be the children."

—Herbert Kohl
May 2014

What teachers requested

What the principal ordered

What central office designed

What was manufactured

What maintenance installed

What the children wanted

Introduction

Education in America is in trouble, again. That is the take-off point for this book. As a way out of the educational morass that state and federal officials have created these past 30 or more years, I propose what may seem like an unorthodox solution to our problems—one that, hopefully, will come to be seen as a real, vital and necessary proposition. *I propose to go back and capture what happened to teaching and learning in the 1960s and 1970s, to understand what innovative educators did then and to apply this knowledge to today's schools.*

Sometimes, a personal journey mirrors the movement of the larger society. It can also be a lamp which throws light on that history. Without seeming immodest, I think my history with traditional, innovative and alternative schools in the late 1960s and beyond is a metaphor for that time in education.

In 1969, Stan Barondes and I established the Teacher Drop-Out Center. Initially, TDOC was located in the School of Education at the University of Massachusetts in Amherst, where the Dean, Dwight Allen, had created a loose, informal climate which supported experimentation by doctoral students and staff.

Stan and I had been high school teachers who had become disenchanted with the low level of curriculum and the teaching methods required by administrators, the same curriculum and methodology that students saw as boring. We were also more than put off by the intolerance toward change in the public schools in the area where we taught just northwest of New York City.

We cared about developing high quality curriculum, we cared about the kids and we cared about linking the two into an electric unity. We talked *with* students, we tried to explore social, moral and intellectual ideas that we and the students were engaged with, we experimented with moving away from lectures by breaking classes into smaller groups and trying hands-on activities and projects. We both got into trouble with our administrators for doing these actions. This was in the middle-to-late 1960s.

So, we dropped out of teaching, sensing that there were others like us yearning to create good learning places for students. (This was about the time that Herb Kohl published a piece in the *New York Review of Books* about the kind of work he was doing with kids in his class in Harlem. Herb later expanded this piece and it was published as *36 Children*.) We thought there must be places for people like us in which to teach. Our vague idea in establishing the Teacher Drop-Out Center was to find these "good places." Also, we hoped to develop a list of people who were, like us, looking for such good schools in which to teach. We thought we could serve as a kind of marriage service—matching specific people with specific schools.

We began to look for good schools. Early on, I contacted John Holt in Boston. John had published *How Children Fail* (a companion book to his *How Children Learn*), which became quite popular, and he was invited all over the country to speak. In his travels, he had come across a number of good schools and had begun to compile a list of them. We contacted these schools for information. People in these schools referred us to more schools. Within a few months, we had put together an annotated list of about two hundred schools.

Most of these were fairly new, small, private, alternative schools. They were modeled after Summerhill, the British Infant Schools which flourished in the '50s and '60s, and Montessori schools. There were Waldorf schools, farm schools, storefront schools, "free" schools, open schools, community schools, urban academies, parent cooperatives, schools-without-walls and schools-within-schools. There were many different kinds of schools with a wide variety of beliefs and practices. What they had in common was a fierce dedication to being student-centered, to high expectations, to teachers working closely with kids, with personalizing learning and with being communities of learners—all of which were aspects of our definition of a good school.

We found these schools in many places, though most were clustered in or near New York City, northern New Jersey, Cambridge/Boston, Philadelphia, Seattle, Berkeley and San Francisco. Most of these schools were on the East and West coasts, though there were a number in St. Paul/Minneapolis, Chicago, East Lansing and connected (directly or indirectly) to colleges and universities. Others were sprinkled about the country, though there were not many in the South or the Southwest.

We discovered a world of excitement in these "new" schools—an excitement generated by a closeness between adults and students in environments where teachers were given the freedom and the responsibility to try out their ideas. We soon found that the number of these schools was growing monthly. By the middle '70s, our list had expanded to over 3,000 of such schools.

When we had developed our initial list in 1969 and early 1970, we mailed out information to schools about TDOC and asked them to list their open positions with us. We began a modest newsletter that profiled schools and announced our services.

TDOC became widely known quickly. Newspapers and magazines wrote about us and we appeared on radio and TV programs. We were deluged with letters from teachers who wanted information about student-centered schools. Most of these were painful letters that told of teachers' struggles to try out new ideas in their classrooms and of the bureaucracies that stifled them.

We did serve as a sort of marriage broker for a few months, matching teachers and schools, but the sheer volume of teachers looking for good schools forced us to abandon these efforts.

We started to list the positions in our newsletter and to charge a small fee for it since we were graduate students without any income and families to support. We also published articles about these "new" schools: about how they were structured, how they worked, how teachers taught, curriculum and studies they did, how they solved legal problems, who their students were and other similar issues. We wrote about materials, books and resources for teachers and schools. Soon, we were getting articles from teachers, administrators, parents and students, which we published. People like John Holt and Jonathan Kozol gave us articles.

Indeed, it was a time when a number of educational writers became famous and most of them became our friends. These included the previously mentioned John Holt, Herb Kohl and Jonathan Kozol, but also included George Dennison, Paul Goodman, Bea and Ron Gross, Deborah Meier, Neil Postman, Miriam Wasserman, Patricia Montgomery and Nat Hentoff.

This was a heady time for Stan and me. It was a time of great educational excitement: everything that was part of the traditional, accepted educational system was being questioned and confronted. Why should we all teach the same thing? Why does curriculum have to be standardized? Can't there be standards without standardization? Since each school is unique, shouldn't all schools be R & D centers? Are there other ways to teach reading besides using basals? Shouldn't schools *personalize* learning? Why do kids have to sit in rows and be talked at by an adult standing in front of the room or sitting at her desk? Can the style of teaching be matched to the student's style of learning? Is it possible to have classrooms where students work cooperatively using materials and projects? Why are classes single graded? How can curriculum be integrated? Does school have to occur in a building? Are there alternatives to testing and grading? Who can be teachers? What should be studied? Should the range of subject matter be traditionally thin and narrow or could it be infinitely expansive and deep, as the world is? Should children be required to attend school and classes? Can students be involved in school decision-making? Why can't parents be partners in all school decision-making? Is it possible to meld these alternative schools into some sort of national movement to change all of education?

Of course, this questioning was happening in the midst of *The Crisis in the Classroom* and *The Greening of America*, within larger social movements, as is often the case with education.

Much of this questioning focused on pedagogical issues, while some school reformers confronted the sociological functions of traditional education: making children loyal and well-functioning members of society, while serving as sorting institutions.

The Teacher Drop-Out Center was right in the middle of this new energy around the re-thinking of schooling. The time was something like the Progressive School Movement in the 1890 – 1930 period. Indeed, one of the exciting things for "new" schools people in the '60s and '70s was discovering the books, the people and the schools from that time and seeing the parallels with our own period. In some ways, it was the second coming of the progressive schools.

In hindsight, it is clear that this was more like a mini-second coming. In the '60s and '70s, some people spoke about an "alternative schools movement," but it was not really a movement since it affected no more that 1% - 2% of the America's student population and since it lasted for about 12 to 15 years. It seemed counter productive that schools which already had gained freedom and achieved great diversity would want to become a "movement". Still, what happened in many of these innovative classrooms and schools was profound. *That is why it is important for us to go back and to recover what was learned then, to understand the questions and the various answers and to see if this will get us out of our current muddle of schooling.*

TDOC helped to organize conferences about alternative schools. Of course, these were informal—ones that were quite different from the traditional conference of present-a-paper, with one or two responders and a question-and-answer session. Ours were more like fairs, with face-painting, music, home-cooked meals, "new" games, interactive talks and community-type meetings which involved adults and students. It was a time for sharing among people involved with or interested in these innovative schools.

We also helped individuals and groups to develop student-centered schools.

While we were establishing TDOC on the East Coast, unknown to us, a similar group was forming on the West Coast. They called themselves the New Schools Exchange and they began to publish a newsletter, similar to ours, but more "professional" looking. We were literally mirroring each other's activities. We made contact with the people at NSE in the early '70s, but we never really worked together.

By the middle 1970s, there were about a dozen small, alternative school journals and newsletters being published around the country. Each of these publications became a local center of information and activism about school change. Except for TDOC, NSE Newsletter and *Changing Schools* (out of the University of Indiana), these publications were short-lived, mirroring the schools themselves.

Many of the alternative schools from that time died out fairly quickly. They died out for many reasons—lack of money, poor implementation of ideas, weak leadership, starry-eyed teachers, political pressures and the like. Also, my sense, based on first-hand knowledge, was that some of these alternative schools were not very good.

When explorers go into a new territory, no one has gone ahead to mark the trees so it is not unusual to make a wrong turn or to get lost. The important point is to find your way out, to learn from the wrong turn taken. And that's what happened for many of us who were involved with "new" schools.

Also, the good schools—for example, the Cambridge (MA) Alternative Public School; Dave Lehman's Community School in Ithaca, NY; Herb Snitzer's Lewis-Wadhams School in mid-New York state; Deborah Meier's Central Park East in NYC; the St. Paul Open School; Margaret Skutch's Early Learning Center in Stamford, CT; Patricia Carini's Prospect School, Burlington, VT; and Pat Montgomery's Clonlara in Ann Arbor, MI —were very good indeed. You would not want to send your child anywhere else once you saw them.

For those readers who want to learn more about what a school was like during that time, I'd recommend reading George Dennison's *The Lives of Children*, probably the best book from that period. It tells the story of a small learning center in NYC. Actually, it is the story of a John Dewey/Paul Goodman inspired teacher and the kids he taught. For those who want a wider view of what was happening with these new schools then, I'd recommend Allen Graubard's *Free the Children: Radical Reform and the Free School Movement* (1973).

In 1971, I moved to New Jersey to start and run a teacher education program at Stockton State College, a few miles west of Atlantic City. Simultaneously, I established the Atlantic County New School, a K-8, multi-graded, open classroom school, loosely connected to the college, which I initially started for my own children. I also directed a state-wide network of public and private alternative schools.

Alternative *public* schools were established early on. That's where the children were and that's where the possibility of sustained funding was. People felt the power of ideas from the private, student-centered schools and wanted similar ones in the public sector.

Obviously, these innovative public schools sprang up in the same areas where there were private ones: in and around New York City, Cambridge/Boston, Seattle, Philadelphia, Berkeley, St. Paul/Minneapolis and San Francisco.

By the middle '70s, with funding from the federal Department of Education, a number of these cities had established a network of alternative schools. Most prominent were those in Berkeley, San Francisco, St. Paul/Minneapolis and Seattle. Even smaller cities like Cambridge, MA, and Montclair, NJ, developed a system of choice as the basis for their public schools. The concept of neighborhood schools was abolished and in its place parents could choose from a variety of different kinds of schools.

Like the private schools, these public alternatives were incredibly varied: open schools with multi-graded classrooms, Montessori schools, free schools, schools-without-walls, fundamental or back-to-basics schools, E. D. Hirsch "Core Knowledge" schools, schools-within-schools and the like. There were traditional schools where one or two teachers were trying new ideas, in the same way that Herb Kohl had done a few years earlier. Some, like the Angier School (Newton, MA), developed an open classroom sequence along with the traditional set of graded classrooms under the leadership of Roland Barth, who a few years later founded the Principal's Center at the Harvard Graduate School of Education, with a handful of other area principals (including me) helping him.

But there were differences between the private and public alternative schools. The latter were mostly small schools, but they were still larger than most private ones. The fervor and radicalism lessened and changed, though groups in urban areas seized the opportunity to assert community control over schools in their neighborhoods. Of course, most of us remember Oceanhill-Brownsville in NYC and how it became famous as parents struggled with the Board of Education and the American Federation of Teachers for control of their schools. Such struggles occurred in many cities. For example, TDOC was instrumental in helping a group of parents gain control of the Adams School in Washington, DC. We also found them a principal and a number of teachers. Next door, we worked with the Morgan district as it became community controlled and chose Ken Haskins as its principal.

By the middle '70s, cities began using innovative schools as "magnets" to help desegregate their public schools. (This was another turn in the continuing use of public alternative schools for other than just educational reasons. From their beginnings, alternative schools were political, like charter schools today.) These types of magnet schools—supported by federal, state and local funds—spread rapidly. Thousands of these magnets grew up all over the country in cities large and small: in Boston, MA; Hartford, CT; Chicago, IL; and Rochester, NY, for example.

Massachusetts established a very strong racial balance law which financially supported the development of a system of "controlled choice" and magnet schools as a way for districts to achieve racial balance. (A parent could choose whatever public school s/he wanted, regardless of neighborhood, just as long as there was space and racial balance was maintained, along with transportation.) Cambridge was the first district to establish this controlled choice system in the early '80s and it is still in operation there now. (The plan was based on the city-wide Cambridge Alternative Public School, founded by a group of parents in 1972, before the concept of magnets existed. I became principal of CAPS in 1974. CAPS evolved into the Graham & Parks Alternative Public School in 1981. For a detailed analysis of this process and this remarkable school, see my *Making an Extraordinary School: The Work of Ordinary People*.) Each of the K-8 schools in the district was encouraged to become a "magnet," to attract students by distinguishing itself in some way. Some did. So, now there are three open-classroom schools, a two-way bilingual school, an E. D. Hirsch school, a Montessori school and an inclusion school for parents to choose from, in addition to several traditional schools which are evolving distinct identities. Almost a dozen other districts in the state developed similar, controlled choice programs.

The establishment of "alternative" schools for "special" students was an ominous appropriation by many public school districts. Kids who caused problems, potential or actual dropouts and special needs students, were isolated off into separate, "alternative" programs. This appropriation became so pervasive that the word "alternative" is now understood by most public school educators to mean these "special" schools for these "special" groups of students.

I see this as a co-option of the entire notion of alternative schools. It is a perversion of one of the mains goals of many such schools: to have a balanced group of students—balanced by race, gender, social-economic backgrounds, styles of learning and age. The idea is to have a good school for all kinds of children.

I think that the starting point for learning in a democracy has to be with a balanced, heterogeneous group of students. From this starting point, a school can begin to grapple with other structures: how to get these diverse children to work together across the usual barriers of race, gender and socio-economic backgrounds; how to establish curricula that actively engages adults and children in high quality moral, intellectual and social issues as well as in basic skills; how to work out decision-making processes that involve everyone—staff, students and parents; and how to establish teaching and learning practices that are consonant with democratic ideals.

We do not know how a child learns. This truism accounts for just about everything that's ever happened in education—the great variety of philosophies of education and the same great variety in approaches to teaching and learning. Actually, these multiple responses are mostly variations of two main reactions.

The first has been a conservative response and it goes like this: since we do not know how kids learn, it then behooves us to look at what we do know—what's been "tried and true" and traditionally passed down—and use what seems to work best. The way No Child Left Behind states this is to tell educators to use "best practices" garnered from "scientific research," reinforced with a series of "high stakes tests," followed by "sanctions." Mandated curriculum, standards and tests were initially established in each state in the 1990s and early 2000s, and these are now being replaced by "common core" National Standards, with support and pressure from the federal Department of Education and its Race To The Top agenda with the carrot of millions of dollars.

The second type of response from educators has been to begin with what seems to have worked best in the past (especially the more progressive practices) and then to try out new ideas, new subject matter and new methods in order to see how teaching and learning can be improved. Often, practically every assumption about traditional schooling is eventually challenged in this approach.

This is how a fair number of administrators and teachers acted in the 1960s and 1970s. When I was principal of an alternative public school, we often thought of our school as an R&D center since we were all constantly trying out new ideas and practices, always seeking to make a better experience for our children. Actually, this was one of the major reasons for the school's success: there was an excitement about trying to improve practice, trying out new ideas, teachers talking with each other about new ideas, pushing and challenging each other to get better. Thousands of visitors often commented on the positiveness and the high energy in the school.

Bush's NCLB and Obama's RTTT empowered state

and federal governments to establish and develop standards, expectations and curriculum. Progressive educators believe in empowering individuals and small groups to educate children, believe in personalized education, believe in joining the curriculum with the needs of the child. Obviously, the gap between these two perspectives is vast.

Even some educators who are skeptical about the efficacy of NCLB contend that it has had positive effects. For example, test scores are now reported for subgroups so that the performance of minority and white children can be compared, the learning levels of special needs children can be easily seen and the test scores of children of poverty can be compared to middle class children's scores. Previously, scores for an entire school or grade were reported and there was no public way to see the gaps in achievement among these various groups, though I would contend that it was relatively easy at that time to look at individual scores and to make accurate deductions and conclusions about a sub-group's performance. We did it all of the time.

These same educators point also to NCLB/RTTT's support and promulgation of standards, making it clear to all teachers what they must expect children to learn and to achieve. I agree with this point though I would note that the standards movement existed prior to NCLB and was seen by most educators as a positive step. I also disagree with how the federal and state governments have mandated standards, taking away teachers' and schools' involvement in their development. I contend that we need standards but we do not need standardization.

My experience has been that people do not thrive under bureaucratic directives because they do not own any part of what they are being told to implement, are not responsive to the big club of high stakes tests, to public shaming when scores are published in local newspapers, to being sanctioned and put "on watch" or "in corrective action," or to educators' pay linked to these same dubious tests.

When teachers, administrators, parents and students have control over what they do, are a part of developing their school community, then they will thrive: they will own what they are building, will want to make their school a high quality place, because control and freedom are the bases on which ordinary people can build an extraordinary community of learners.

*****

The main idea in this book is to show why it is vitally important for educators and others concerned with schooling in America today to go back to the 1960s and 1970s. Why go back 30 or 40 years? Haven't we moved way beyond what happened back then?

I'm not encouraging us to abandon our computers for typewriters and mimeograph machines. I don't want anyone to take a sentimental journey back to "the good old days." I'm advocating for a close, critical scrutiny of schooling today—as I have done briefly above—and then to take these same critical eyes back to examine the realities then: what did educators espouse and what did they put into practice? What was life like for kids in schools then? Can we capture the spirit of those who established and worked in the best student-centered schools?

I think learning the what's, how's and why's of education in the '60s and '70s will position us to move beyond the failures of schooling in America today, failures best exemplified by the No Child Left Behind Act and the current Race To The Top.

As I noted above, NCLB has been a focused juggernaut that's become the dominate force in education, obliterating much of the past and putting in place the worst aspects of traditional schooling. Most educators today, especially new teachers, know only prescribed curriculum, state standards and constant testing. Teachers and administrators are leaving the field in unprecedented numbers, driven out by the intolerant, mean-spirited and narrowness of the law and what it causes schools and teachers to do, which is to organize almost everything around passing high stakes tests.

More and more people are coming to realize that NCLB is bankrupt. Test scores may be rising, but there has been scant corroboration from assessments outside of the closed circle of high stakes, state-mandated tests. What we have seen are testing gains, not learning gains. Prominent educators like Howard Gardner, Roland Barth, Eleanor Duckworth and Jonathan Kozol are speaking out strongly against the law. Ask college professors if students are coming to class better prepared now than ten years ago; ask those employers hiring recent high school grads if they come with more skills and knowledge than previous generations of students. You will find few who will say that students have made the large academic gains that testing scores seem to indicate.

In an article on reading in *The New Yorker* (Dec. 24 & 31, 2007), Caleb Crain reports that the federal "Department of Education found that reading skills have improved moderately among fourth and eighth graders in the last decade and a half, with the largest jump occurring just *before* the No Child Left Behind Act took effect..."

The National Center for Educational Statistics reported in 2006 that only 70% of U. S. students graduated from high school in four years, and in low-income communities the average was closer to 50%. Of those who go on to college, 40% require remediation and 46% fail to graduate in six years.

A from-the-bottom ground swell is starting to emerge against NCLB/RTTT. Reacting to this criticism, the Obama administration has offered exemptions to some of the law's rules and regulations while some in the Republican Party are calling for less federal involvement in education, though their aim is to privatize public education.

Further evidence can be seen in the large crowds that are

currently attending the numerous screenings of the film "Race to Nowhere" all over the country and the discussions which follow where parents, students and teachers affirm and verify how deadly the system has become.

Today, a third of new teachers leave the profession within three years and half leave within five years. This amazing statistic takes me full circle to the '60s and the reason that we established the Teacher Drop-Out Center. Teachers are leaving behind their careers because they feel powerless in a system which does not honor their intelligence, they are feed up with teaching standardized curriculum, feel demeaned by having to constantly teach to "the test" and experience the daily degradation from state and national legislators and the general public.

If not NCLB, then what? The explosion of ideas and activities in the 1960s and 1970s came after a long period of decaying traditionalism in American education. I think that something similar will happen in the near future. Educators will shuffle off NCLB/RTTT and they will be looking for better ways. That's why I propose going back to the '60s and '70s: to learn about what was developed during that vibrant time and to seek guidance on how we might move forward. It was, indeed, an exciting time, a time when many ordinary educators tried many different things, questioned just about everything concerning teaching and learning. This experimentation resulted in a great explosion of learning. After our current, conservative period, this is exactly what educators will need to do, too.

Schooling does not exist in a vacuum. Educators and their schools exist in a larger social framework and what happens in that larger setting is directly connected to schooling. So, when we go back to the '60s and '70s, we also, necessarily, will go back to what was happening in America at large then. The large social movements were captured in the most influential book from that period, Charles A. Reich's *The Greening of America* (1970).

Reich summarized that time in the following sentence: "It must be understood in the light of the betrayal and loss of the American dream, the use of the Corporate State of the 1960s and the way in which that State dominates, exploits, and ultimately destroys both nature and man." Most people will acknowledge that these conditions are much worse today than back then.

The large social movements of the 1960s that spilled into the '70s were people's attempts at confronting that State (and most centers of authority), attempts at restoring the balance of power back to individuals, re-connecting us as individuals and re-building a true sense of community among us, building democracy, and confronting exploitative consumerism—attempts at developing a "new man/new woman" who would practice egalitarianism and social justice. Schools were seen as an important locus of this quest.

The rationale behind Bush's NCLB and Obama's Race To The Top is that we need to educate our children better so that America can win the world's economic competition. The driving force behind the innovations and reforms of the '60s and '70s was supporting the growth of children. For most, there was also the goal of developing schools that exemplified and promoted democracy.

Today's educators need to examine all aspects of schooling, in spite of the pressure not to. They need to understand the purposes of schooling, how children learn, the various ways a classroom and lessons can be structured, the roles of children and adults in the learning process, who can serve as teachers, who should own the curriculum, what defines high quality work, what can be taught and the relationships among and between children and adults. This is what happened in the '60s and '70s and it would serve us well to go back and see how educators then did this same kind of scrutiny and what they learned. It would certainly make the work we need to do much easier.

The essays in this book are *personal* since they come directly out of my experiences during the 1960s and 1970s: observing my own children learning, reflecting on my learning, teaching, running a private, alternative school, running a teacher education program, observing many schools, starting an international organization to promote and support innovative schools, being an educational consultant and being the principal of a public, alternative school.

What I've also tried to do is to use these personal experiences as a spring board, as the basis for understanding the nature of schooling in America and the broader issues of teaching and learning, including justice and community, in our culture. Thus, the essays may start out being personal but they ray out into the larger, public issues facing education, becoming less personal as the book unfolds.

Some of the chapters are not only personal, but they are written as narratives because I've tried to make what was happening with education in the '60s and '70s accessible, to make it come alive.

So, this is a heads-up to the reader: The form of the book is quite different from most books on education, but I think this unconventional approach fits perfectly with its ideas and will be easily understood.

Now, I invite you to go back with me and re-live teaching and learning in the 1960s and 1970s.

Chapter 1
He Often Creates Out of His Fullness

When my son was four, he asked me to buy him a model car. Thoughts ran through my head and the teacher in me said: He usually breaks apart the things that we buy him and now he'd be putting something together. I think it would be good for him and he'd probably learn a lot from the experience. It'd also probably be fun. So, I said, "Okay I think it's a good idea. We'll buy you the model car tomorrow."

Later that evening, my wife said I should not have promised to buy him the car. It could be too hard for a child to assemble. She said she was afraid that if Lenny was given something too complicated to do he might get frustrated and become adverse to dealing with complexities later on, and maybe he'd even come to somehow secretly dislike me.

I thought she was exaggerating and I argued with her, which caused me to be more determined to buy Lenny the model car.

We all went to the store the next evening and Lenny said, "I want to choose it for myself, Dad-dy." And he did. He wouldn't let the checkout clerk wrap it and he clutched it tightly all the way home. He wanted to put it together immediately, in spite of being very tired. He opened the box and I was confronted by a mess, parts and pieces jumbled together, things to be broken off and glued, with extra pieces for alternative designs. I knew I had never put together a model before and I was tired, too.

I didn't have any plastic cement as the directions suggested, so my wife got out some paste glue, but she would not help us. I put a few simple pieces together and then tried to paste the motor parts together. But I couldn't do it. I read the directions quickly, but I still could not understand how to do it. All the while, Lenny and his younger brother, Chris, were playing with the pieces, breaking parts off, mixing them up, trying to put some together, shouting for me to help them, to hurry up, saying the glue was not working. I told them to be quiet, to let the pieces alone and not to mix them up. They didn't and they did. I got angry, but I told Lenny that we didn't have the right kind of glue so we couldn't put the car together tonight. I threw all the parts back into the box and told him we'd finish it when I bought the right kind of glue. He cried, but I put him to bed.

Next morning, I was in the kitchen fixing breakfast when Lenny came running in, face smiling, eyes liquid and wide. "Dad-dy! Dad-dy! Look! I put it togefer!" And he had, sort of. He had found the hub caps, snapped them off the plastic stick holder and put them into the rubber wheels. He was shaking with excitement.

When I saw him standing there holding up the wheels, two memories flashed into my mind:

My father refused to go to a shopping center or to any big store. When he bought anything, he went where he knew the people and where he could haggle over the prices. There were still some stores like this then, especially in poor rural areas like the one where my Dad lived in southwestern Pennsylvania. He liked one store in particular to buy clothes. I don't know why exactly, but one reason is probably that the owner, a small, animated, Lebanese man with a high voice, could speak Slovak. My Dad thought this was amazing since only Slovaks should speak Slovak. Of course, he liked to talk with the old guy in Slovak.

I remembered a day when I was a college freshman and Father was a factory worker, sometimes carpenter and former coal miner, when I drove him to this store so he could buy a pair of work pants.

When we went into the store, we were waited on by a new clerk, the owner evidently was out. Father told the young man what he wanted. The clerk took him to a rack, picked out a pair of slacks and held them up to Dad. "Do you like this style?" he asked. "They're a new line we just got in. The guys in your factory will think you're an executive when you come walking in with these on."

My Father turned white, threw the slacks on the floor and said, "I'm a workin' man. I want some worken pants." And I remembered my reaction, how I tried to hide my embarrassment, all the while that we stood there *until he got his workin' pants.*

When I was a high school teacher, I had one of my classes in a small lecture-auditorium because the school was overcrowded. The rows were elevated and I usually stood at the bottom and leaned back against a rail while the students sat scattered about the room, though most sat close to me.

We had been talking about violence in a Hemingway story, about how some people get enmeshed in the savagery they're afraid of, when a memory came to the front of my head and I told the class about it.

When I was about thirteen, a few friends and I decided to trap muskrats to make some money from selling the furs. (That's when muskrat furs were popular.) One morning I was out alone checking the traps, when I came upon a possum caught in one of my traps. It was alive, chewing away at its clamped leg in an attempt to free itself. I had a handle from a shovel with me, the wood hard and smooth. I tried to kill the possum with it.

I hit the possum on the head. It felt like hitting a snow bank, the club sinking silently into the possum's white fur. It just sat there and stared at me with its black eyes.

I hit it again and then again, harder and harder, raising the club like an axe, but it wouldn't die. I tried holding its head under the icy water with the club, but it still wouldn't die. So I beat it and beat it, blood splattering over my arms and legs, holding its head under water with my boots, stomping it, hitting and pounding it with the club until I was shaking all over and its head and snout were a bloody mess and it was dead without muttering a sound.

I had forgotten the class in the telling, leaning forward and gripping the chair in front of me, staring straight ahead. When I looked up, I saw Nadine, a student, sitting on the edge of her chair, eyes watery. She looked at me and then started to speak.

She had been a counselor in a camp that previous summer and there was one little boy who bugged her. He wouldn't listen to her and he often defied her. One day the kid had disobeyed her and somehow hurt another boy and Nadine got angry. The boy saw her face and ran. She ran after him, knocked him down and began hitting him. She hit him and hit him and didn't hear him screaming until another counselor pulled her off the boy.

Nadine sat there staring down at me and tried to tell me what she felt when she hit the boy. She sat there with tears in her eyes and tears came into my eyes but I was at the bottom and Nadine near the top row and the bell had rung and I had cafeteria duty to go to.

These memories came flooding up the back of my mind like the headlights of a car over an approaching hill on a dark night and it came to me that learning is living—a stasis, sometimes a sinking, a troubled gathering of the sap of our stored being, joys shooting up through the growing pains. And there was Lenny, standing there holding up those wheels.

I had often thought that people create out of their

loneliness, but I discovered that they often create out of their fullness, too.

We went back into the living room and started putting the model car together. My wife was right in some ways. The car *was* complicated, but we went slowly, found good glue in my tool box and put the model together. We looked at each piece, played with them, tried to figure out where each went. It took us several days to glue the model, working when we felt like it, but, before we were through, my wife and Chris, our other son, were also helping us with it.

Now, we have a model car. Though pieces are missing, some broken, some badly glued, some in the wrong places, it is together.

Chapter 2
Oh, Wow, Dad-dy, I Know My Alphabets

While I was lying propped up in bed reading the newspaper, Lenny came in and stood by the bed. He put a red piece of cardboard on my belly and said, "Dad-dy, write my name."

I said, "O.K.," and reached for a pen on the nightstand.

He said, "No. Write it with a pen-cil." I told him that the pencil would not show up well on the dark red, but he insisted, so I started to print out his first name. He couldn't see it, so he asked me to use the pen. I printed out **LEONARD**, saying each letter aloud, saying the word phonetically, and was about to write the last name when he said, "Write *all* my names."

I printed out **LEONARD JOSEPH SOLO, JUNIOR**. He turned the card over and asked me to write all his brother's names. I printed out **CHRISTOPHER LYN SOLO**, saying each letter as I slowly formed them in block letters. Lenny took the card and looked it over carefully and then started to run out of the room. He stopped suddenly and said, "I have a *C* in my name."

I was puzzled because I knew he could recognize his name. The previous week he had asked his mother for a piece of paper and a pen, sat down at the kitchen table, and wrote **LoeEa LOEADo**, with squiggly lines. He also wears a name tag at nursery school and he can pick his out of the pile in the morning for the student-teachers to pin it on his back.

I told him, "No, Lenny, you don't have a *C* in your name."

He evidently thought the *J* was a *C* since I had printed it a bit sloppily and it looked somewhat like a backward *C*. I told him *Joseph* started with a *J*.

Lenny's face fell into a frown and he said, "*C* starts in *see-saw*."

"No, Lenny, *see-saw* starts with an *S*." He turned his face from me and ran out of the room.

I laid there and thought about a curious poem he'd made the previous week. My wife and I had bought the children a toy guitar and Lenny likes to sit and strum it, occasionally making up songs. I overheard him singing and wrote down the words:

> When I was reading my book,
> My flower grew so big
> I had to run and kill it,
> to run and kill my flower.

I was amazed and so I printed it out in big letters and taped it on the kitchen wall. We have all sorts of other things taped and stapled on the wall from the children: paintings, Sesame Street posters, drawings, pastings, alphabet letters that the kids have printed or traced on their own, and the like.

I've since seen Lenny in the kitchen running his fingers over the letters (making me regret that I had not made them out of sandpaper or felt), saying them, trying to repeat his poem, always doing it with new variations.

This is an interesting thing I've seen with kids. When you ask them to repeat a story or a poem they've made up, it is always different, new things added, other details dropped, a kind of minstrel-like reliance on the spoken rather then the written word.

Lenny came back into the room with a piece of tape on the cardboard and hung it on the wall. He crawled up onto the bed beside me and said, "*See-saw* starts with a *C*." He had been trying hard on his own to puzzle out the letters and sounds and he evidently thought he knew the *C* letter and its sound.

"No, Lenny, it starts with an *S*. Here, I'll write it on the paper. Sometimes *C*- and *S*-words sound alike. It's hard." But he grabbed my hand and wouldn't let me write it, scowled, and insisted that the word began with a *C*. I told him to go out into the kitchen and check the Sesame Street alphabet poster. He ran out and was back up on the bed in a few moments.

I held his hand and said, " *See-Saw's* a hard word, Lenny, because of how it sounds. Here, let me write it out for you now, OK?" I printed it out and then he traced the letters with his fingers. I asked him to find a *C* in the newspaper and he found one in a headline. Then, I asked him to write one. He tried but finally said, "I don't know how to do it, Dad-dy." So, I printed one for him and he printed a very shaky one beside it.

He jumped off the bed and ran out into the living room and came jumping back up onto the bed. He had a cardboard letter *C* with him, taken from one of the sets we have in boxes around the apartment, and he proceeded to trace it in the newspaper's margin. I told him to go check the red card he had taped onto the wall and he went over, turned the card around and shouted, "*Christopher* starts with a *C*!"

When he got back on the bed, I asked him to make an *O* with his pencil. He knows this letter and made one quickly. Then, I erased part of it and asked him what it was. He smacked himself on the forehead, shouted, "It's a *C*!" and fell back smiling in a pretend faint.

I asked him to make another *O*. He did and then I put my hand on his and guided the pencil to put a slash line at the bottom of the letter. He smacked his forehead again, shouted, "A *Q*!" and went through the same fainting routine.

I asked him if he wanted to try some "more hard letters." He said, "Yesss. Oh, wow, Dad-dy, I know my alphabets now!" and he gave me a hard hug.

Another person probably would have done different things

at this point: a phonics teacher would have sounded out letters in words, a Sylvia Ashton-Warner would have searched for "organic words," a Caleb Gattagno would have gotten Lenny into words and colors and a Maria Montessori would have cut out felt or sandpaper letters. In other contexts, I may have done some of these things, too, but Lenny and I just continued to play around with letters.

He made another *C*. When he did, I added a line to it and he immediately recognized it as a *G*. We did a few other "really hard letters, Dad-dy." I made a *V* and asked him to tell me a word that began with it. He jumped down from the bed, ran out into the kitchen and came running back in and said, "I want to tell you a secret in your ear."

He whispered in my ear, "*Violin* starts with a *V*!"

"Really?"

"Yes, it really does," he said, clapping his hands and smiling. Evidently, he'd found the letter, word and picture on the Sesame Street poster. I wrote out the word for him. Then, I made another *V* and put a straight line at the bottom of it, but he did not recognize it as a *Y*. We looked through the paper and he was able to find a *Y* in an advertisement, along with a *J* in the word *Jack* in the same ad.

We messed around with some more interesting letters: *U* and *V*; *W* and *M*; *H* and *A* (in block letter form); *P*, *R* and *B* ("*B* with a big fat belly"); *i* and *l* and *L*, noting the differences between large and small letters, finding them in the newspaper, Lenny drawing legs and eyes on some of the *O*'s.

Then, my wife shouted that supper was ready and Lenny and I walked hand-in-hand to the kitchen. I thought about all the things that must have come together for him. Deanna, my wife, and I had never taught him the alphabet or, more accurately, never made him memorize it and repeat it in a sing-songy way. We have various alphabet posters hanging in several rooms, boxes of alphabets are scattered around the house, there's a shelf of books that he looks at irregularly, we read to him daily, Lenny watches Sesame Street and the Electric Company religiously, and he goes to a nursery school at the local university. But, as he says, he "just plays" at this school, a loosely structured Montessori / Integrated Day affair, hardly ever going into the more structured learning area. No one had taught him the alphabet, yet here he was learning it.

He was learning it at home and not at school. Now, that was an irony for me: learning at home and playing at school. Then, I realized this thought was a bit ridiculous because school should be a place for kids to play, a place for human relationships in a rich, loving atmosphere, a warm extension of the home, a place where a child is treated as an individual, with dignity and care, and education is personalized. I realized, too, that a home had to be an organic extension of the school, that learning isn't confined to a special building called a school between the hours of 8:30 and 2:30. To isolate learning to a school is as absurd as isolating love to a home.

I know there are not many schools like the one my son attends—especially public ones—but small, student-centered schools are growing up everywhere with the recent rise in the number of innovative and alternative schools.

I don't mean that I want the world to be thought of as just one large school with people conspiring and manipulating the environment so that a child's every action is a planned "learning experience."

I visited a nationally franchised Learning Center recently and the director pointed the fancy playground equipment out to me and explained how these were meant "to develop the large muscles." I told him that my kids played football with their friends and climbed trees. A child's world should not be bereft of the natural, the messy, the unexpected and the random.

What I do mean is that learning is living and living is (or should be) learning, but all of life does not have to be planned and organized by adults as a form of learning because kids learn in the most odd, erratic, episodic, unexpected, individual and amazing way... My wife was shaking my shoulder.

"Len, Len." My wife jolted me out of these thoughts. I had been sitting at the supper table utterly oblivious of my family.

I told Deanna what had happened with Lenny and the letters.

"Wow, Lenny, did you really learn all that today?"

"Really, Mommy. I really do know my alphabets now." He looked at us with his shy smile, nodding his head "yes," and held out a hand to each of us and we held them, the whole family joined in his joy.

Chapter 3
Beard with Holes

Several thousand innovative and alternative schools grew up in this country during the 1960s and 1970s. There are a number of books that describe these new schools and each seems to be saying, "Here's our school. We are not a 'free' school. Summerhill is in England and this is New England. This is the First Street School, this is the School in Rose Valley and that's the New School for Children. We're each different, unique, as all good schools are."[1]

One of the commonalities among these reports is that many of the founders of these schools were individuals who were strong and quietly confident, women and men who had visions that grew out of but went beyond themselves, whose heads were in the clouds but whose feet were in the mud, people who knew basically what they wanted to see happen and were, in Bob Dylan's words, "busy being born." They worked long and hard with other adults at helping small numbers of children learn. They were hustlers, opportunists, and entrepreneurs who operationalized their visions, sometimes like guerrilla fighters.

Margaret Skutch was such an individual and she wrote a book, *To Start a School*, about her Early Learning Center (ELC) in Stamford, Connecticut. I am not going to review the book directly but I will review it indirectly by describing a visit to the school. I had been there several times previously and I returned to supervise some college students I had placed there as interns. The building was more than interesting. It was round, with lots of windows, and the plumbing, electricity and heating showed on the inside so that the students could study how it was made. Inside, one large, open room took up most of the space. I should note that this was before two associates of John Holt helped to create a part of the school into a multi-leveled area of holes, rooms, ramps and equipment arranged so a child could have a fantastic voyage into himself and the world, similar to what they had done to the Shady Lane School in Pittsburgh.

After I was greeted and introduced to some of the staff, I wandered around the various learning areas in the school. I knelt down to examine some mathematical games when I looked up and saw a little girl come walking slowly across the room to a little boy within earshot of me. She said to him in a tiny voice, "Will you be my friend today?"

"Yes," he said and they went off together to the dress-up area to play. That was more than a happy way for me to begin the day.

I sat down on the carpeted floor and took a box of wooden cylinders off a low shelf—homemade shelves of concrete blocks with brightly painted boards strung between them. As I was dumping them out, a small blonde girl came over and sat down beside me. "What're you doing?" she asked. I told her I was "just playing around."

She took a few of the other boxes of cylinders off the shelf and started stacking them up, seeing how high she could build them. She was careful and deliberate, putting the larger cylinders on the bottom and arranging them in order of size. I asked her how old she was and she said, "Four. My name's Mary and I have a baby brother. He's just two," holding up four and then two fingers. She continued piling up the cylinders, taking some of mine, until they were just as tall as she when the stack collapsed. She jumped and clapped her hands, smiling, threw her arms around my neck in a boney hug and sat down in my lap.

I cradled her in my arms and talked with her for a few minutes until she looked up and said, "Let's play shapes."

"Okay," I said and we raced, crawling, to a nearby shelf and got a large box with an assortment of geometrical shapes in it. Mary took out each one, telling me which ones she knew, asking me the names of others: cylinder, "with a circle on each end"; triangle, "with three sides—one, two, three"; rectangle, with "one, two, three, four sides"; etc., while running her fingers over the sides of each shape. We then played around with the pieces for a while, matching the sides up with thin plywood shapes, building houses and just stacking them up.

All of a sudden, a little dark-haired girl came running over and knocked down the stack, scattering the shapes. She grabbed me hard around the neck, faced me, pulled my beard and laughed loudly. She sat down on my lap, then Mary did the same. We sat there and talked for a few moments and I learned her name was Ann, but I felt uncomfortable with her. She was restless, pulling my face down to hers, fidgeting, smiling wanly. Sue, one of my student teachers in the school, came over then and Mary got up and asked me to play with the shapes again. Ann wanted to play, too, and so Sue joined us and we gathered up the scattered pieces.

Ann and Mary made houses out of the boxes and shapes for a while. Then, we again stacked them, counted them, identified them and matched the sides with the flat plywood shapes. Ann knocked my stack down, took pieces from our piles and wanted to build hers higher than anyone's. Mary showed her how to stack them with the larger ones on the bottom, but Ann rushed and her pile kept tumbling down. She then spied an old cloth purse on a shelf and brought it over. We dumped all the pieces into the bag and Sue made up several games.

We first took turns, reaching into the bag, pulling out a shape and identifying it. We then said what kind of shape we were going to get, reached into the bag with our eyes closed and fished around until we found the figure. Both of these went well, all of us interested. Sue suggested we reach into the bag, pick up a figure, describe it, and the other three of us had to identify it from the description. She went first but her description was long and somewhat complicated and neither of the girls knew what she was describing.

Ann grabbed the bag and told me to put my hand in it. When I did, she pulled the drawstrings tight and laughed. I got my hand out and told her not to do that again. Eric, another student, joined us at this point, bringing blocks of wood and sets of wheels which fit together to make cars. Ann and Eric went off to play with these, Sue went outside with some boys and girls, and Mary asked me to read her a story.

We went over to the book corner and Mary rummaged around until she found a book she wanted to read. She sat on my lap and I read the book to her, dramatizing some parts, pointing out letters, spelling words, asking questions, but mostly just reading the story. While I was reading it, Ann came over and quietly sat down on my lap. When I finished the book, both girls wanted to read another book. They looked through the books scattered about, wanting first one, then another, until they both decided on a book that Mary had picked. I read them this one, telling some of the story in simpler words, talking with both, clowning, joking, pointing out letters, words and pictures, asking them questions and mostly just having fun reading the story.

When we finished the book, Mary wanted to go outside, Ann wanted to play dress-up and I wanted to talk with my student teachers, so we went about our separate activities.

One of the regularly organized group activities (which were not required) was at the end of the morning. While things were being cleaned up, the thirty-or-so children would get their coats and boots on, wait for their rides home, and a teacher would do some lessons in a sunken area near the main entrance. This day, a teacher was reading a story and some kids were gathered around her listening and looking at the pictures and words in the book, some sat and talked quietly, some continued to finish up their activities, and some got dressed and went outside to play or just waited around.

In her book, Margaret Skutch makes it clear "that the Early Learning Center is not a place where children bumble from indulgence to indulgence, followed by anxious teachers desperately trying to cope with fifty different demands." The teachers do teach, do organize activities using materials and projects for small groups and individuals, including reading, math, science and the like. But there are times during the day when children can choose what they want to do—use the dress-up corner, the water table, the sand box, the math materials (like multi-based blocks and Cuisenaire rods), the painting area, etc.

I was struck by the sharp contrast between this and a first grade class I had visited in Vermont a week earlier. For some reason, two classes were mixed together that morning. Both teachers were in the room with about fifty children. Some of the kids sat in assigned chairs at low tables on one side of the room and the rest sat on the floor in a line along the wall. The teachers were playing a tape of a man reading a book as one teacher walked around the room holding up the book, level with her face, turning each page, while the other teacher stood by the stereo and watched the children. They were not allowed to talk or move around and the teachers were continuously shushing them as the kids squirmed, squinted, punched, pinched, slid their chairs and talked. I left when the teachers told the kids, "We're all going to do creative dancing now," and then proceeded to line the children up in even rows far apart and told them about the movements they all had to do, all together at the same time.

I wondered what these public school teachers would have done with an event that happened about mid-morning at the

Early Learning Center. One boy in the center of the room began to yell. Then, three or four other children came over and started yelling and obviously all the other students in the school were being interrupted. A teacher quickly went over and asked them to stop, but the kids wanted to scream. So, the teacher said, "All right," and asked if anyone else wanted to join in. Most of the kids wanted to, so they got in a circle in the middle of the room and began to scream and shout at the top of their lungs. The kids were laughing and shouting and it looked like great fun. After a minute or two, everyone was all screamed out and they went back to their activities.

Mrs. Skutch writes about a similar incident, but with a different outcome. A girl was screaming and Margaret asked all the children to join in. "Some did, some didn't. I think a number of children were embarrassed. I think, too, that they knew Ann Louise was screaming about something real, and it wasn't to be made fun of or turned into a game."

Later, I wandered over to a corner where an African-American girl was teaching her little sister the alphabet on a computer. Nearby, some kids were building a little room out of cardboard because they wanted a corner to hide in and a place to go to be alone.

I then walked over to the painting area where Eric was finishing up a book he had made called *Eric's Racing Book*. He had seen an auto race on television that previous weekend, came to school enthused and made a ten or twelve page book about a racing car. He had dictated the story to a teacher who printed it out in dotted-line letters on the right side of the pages. Eric had filled in the letters, painted a car on the cover, and was just about finished making pictures on the left side of each page to correspond with the text on the right. I helped him spread it to finish drying on a rack and, later, helped him staple it together

Mary and Ann came over and I helped them find their paintings. We had a crackers and juice snack, cleaned up the area with a miniature bucket, broom and mop and decided to go listen to a teacher reading a story since school was just about over for the day.

I helped both put on their coats and boots. They sat down on my lap and we listened to the story for a little while. They started playing with my beard, touching the shaved skin areas between my beard and sideburns and said that my "beard had holes in it." I asked them when they were going to get beards and both giggled and told me girls don't have beards. Ann said, "My daddy doesn't have a beard and my mommy has a new baby at home." She asked me if I was going to be at the school the next day. I told her I didn't know because I had a long drive back home, my wife and two kids were expecting me, but the roads were icy. I said that if I could I would come back tomorrow to see her. Her parents came at this point and she went home.

I stayed for lunch with Margaret, the staff and my student teachers as they talked about the day's events and about the children. I talked about Ann and learned why she had been so upset that morning. Ann was disturbed about the recent birth of her brother whom the mother had just brought home from the hospital. The father was away for days, even weeks, on business trips. Before coming over to me this morning, she had scattered a group of alphabet learning materials which a teacher was using with some students and Ann would not let anyone come near her. We talked about ways to deal with the situation: ignore it, role-play a birth scene with Ann as the baby, give more love and attention to Ann, be more firm with her, let the parents know what was happening at school and the like.

The faculty met like this every day. Then, they would have some type of learning activity: weekly Synectics sessions and training in the creative uses of learning materials, whether Montessori materials, materials they had bought from Britain, or materials and projects they had developed alone or together.

The school was well aware that teachers need to learn, too, need supportive structures to look at their practices, to learn from each other and to try out new ideas and materials. Working with children is a difficult, draining job. Also, being only with children for long periods of time is not healthy for a teacher.

Mrs. Skutch had a camera track built into the ceiling of the school, so it can be moved around. She makes videos of teachers and students and then she and the teachers study these to learn more about the children, about how they learn, and to improve their teaching practices. There are several one-way mirrors in the school where an adult can observe and take notes on children and teachers and these are used in the same way to improve instruction.

I visited with the six-to-nine year olds who stayed a full day. This group was an experiment by the school, an attempt to see if its methods could be carried on with these older children.

The kids in this group were developing their own language and they had already accumulated a list of words. When a student came up with a word, s/he cut it out in felt and pasted it on a large board. They were also getting into the process of developing a grammar for the language. Not only was it obviously a lot of fun for the kids, but they were learning a lot about the structure of the English language in the process.

This group was also studying Native Americans and several constructed villages, with a great deal of miniature details like tepees, terrain (rocks, trees, plants, water) and the like. Six year old kids were shaving sticks with sharp knives (which made me anxious, but the kids were careful), others cutting cloth, some molding plaster-like material, all with a casualness that showed me they were quite used to a variety of tools and materials. I didn't have to ask the teacher how these kids learned so much about Native Americans. I could see them working and I heard them talking about Native Americans; there were scores of various books scattered about and it was obvious that they were being read. Additionally, the children had gone to some museums that had exhibits and materials on the several tribes they were studying.

The room this group worked in looked pretty messy, but the kids seemed to thrive in it and knew where everything was among the scattered items. A few days before, some children wanted to know about pendulums so they and a teacher got a plastic water cup, the kind that comes to a point like a cone, filled the cup with paint and suspended it from the ceiling. They cut a small hole in the cup and began experimenting with it, swinging it from various directions and distances, changing the color of the paint and gradually enlarging the hole in the cone, making charts and graphs while doing these various experiments. Not only did they learn about pendulums and their motions, but the room ended up with a neat abstract painting on the concrete floor.

I then spent some time with Margaret Skutch, the directress, and learned about how the school began, its early years in a church basement six or seven years before, its problems and its successes, how she raised money to build the new building and kept the school going, how she adroitly hustled a great deal of equipment, how she hasn't received a salary for years now, the school's legal hassles, the teacher training workshops she conducts, how she found such fine teachers, and about the children in the school and their parents. Most of this is quietly and delicately told in her book.

I talked some more with my student teachers and discovered that they had an extra cot. So, I decided to stay overnight and to go back to the school the next morning. It had been a long and full day.

I do not want to leave the impression that ELC is a "free" school. Mrs. Skutch makes this quite clear:

> I am concerned at the Early Learning Center that freedom should be *for* something. To turn a two-

year old "free" with paint, brushes and papers is to confuse him, perhaps so frustrate him that he will not want to use paints for a long time to come. This is not freedom; it is the most irresponsible laissez-faire, masquerading under the name of "freedom from artificial restrictions and imposed standards." I am not out to restrict or impose. I am out to teach. I can show a child how to use a brush; later, I may suggest that he try out three different ways of using brushes....

I like to see children doing what interests them because they are learning, not because they are little symbols of freedom. When I tell a child that I want him to sit in a certain place or that I can't let him do what he's doing, I don't understand this as a compromise with freedom; I see it as a way of making a better learning situation for all the children, and I do it within what I know and the children know is a real respect for them as free human beings. *Freedom is a way of interacting.*

I also did not want to leave the impression that ELC was perfect. Mrs. Skutch was still heavily influenced by her early Montessori training and this was reflected in the overly tidy, orderly, non-messiness of the younger children's area and in their relatively quiet behavior.

As in nature, I think we must preserve some of the wildness in our children because there are many pressures in our culture that tame and subdue them soon enough.

Stamford was a wealthy community and the cost of attending the school was relatively high. Obviously, a wide variety of children could not attend the school: there were only a few non-white and poor children in the school and most of those attended on scholarships. This led me to a larger issue: ELC was obviously an elitist school. As such, could it really have been a *good* school?

This issue is reflected in the Native American studies I described earlier. There was an antiseptic, neutral quality about the kids' experiences with the materials. There seemed to be none of the kind of talk (or books and resources) that would inspire rage at the exploitation of a race which we took to near extinction but from whose cruel extinction we still profit.

I've mentioned the rise of alternative schools and the attention they have received. In response to an earlier draft of this essay, Jonathan Kozol wrote me to say:

> It has one theme disturbing to me. There are references to Holt, Neill, Dennison and my own work—with little indication that much of what we do is totally incompatible. For example, I adhere to Freire's view that all education involves basic questions of just vs. unjust, not only in the school but in the social order. I don't believe we can take lightly the fact that Neill has run one of the most racist schools in England, steered clear of leftist ideologies, and consequently received great praise and lots of money from the U.S. Holt's non-critical adulation of Neill's work is consistent with his own lifelong involvement with the education of the ruling class. Is our greatest need to make the best a little better or to cut down the disproportion between the worst and best?
>
> The fear of "Movement," voiced by many, is also inconsistent for me with the realistic possibilities of social change on a large scale. To say that I care more about causes than about kids is to side-step the point that to care about kids is to care most of all that they grow up in (and help to construct) an ethical nation.

I agree with Kozol about the necessity for social change on a large scale. It is possible: Gandhi, Mao, Castro, King, Chavez and many others have shown this. But how is this social change best achieved? By politicizing these new schools?

In contrast, I also believe what William James wrote:

> I am done with great things and big things, great institutions and big success, and I am for those tiny, invisible, molecular, moral forces that work from individual to individual, creeping through the crannies of the world like so many soft rootlets, or like the capillary oozing of water, yet which, if you give them time, will rend the hardest monuments of man's pride.

Social change must involve deep, personal changes, changes in individual lives. And here lies the real strength of those who started the new schools. They had strong beliefs. The schools were founded by people who were angry at what many public schools were doing to their children. So, with little or no "professional" advice, they started new schools. They created what Miles Horton calls "islands of decency" in a not-so-decent world. These schools flourished and grew up all over the country in this way: people taking the power into their own hands and building new schools for their children. Many people set up many different kinds of schools: free schools, community schools, open classroom schools, storefront learning centers, schools-without-walls, commune schools, Summerhillian schools, liberation schools, traveling schools, boat-building schools, survival schools, farm schools and on and on.

It was impossible for so many new schools to exist unknown (though it probably would have been to their advantage if they had remained unknown, at least to the large media). Schools found out about each other, visited, held local and national conferences, were elated by the fact that there were so many others like themselves. It appeared as if something basic was happening on a large scale, that a "Movement" was afoot.

First, the counter culture tried to fashion these new schools in its image; then, those who desired large political change wanted to fashion these schools in their image.

Social change is possible, but it is obvious that it will not happen soon or easily. An observer of the failures, the missed revolutions, of the '60s and '70s—social and economic justice, free speech, counter culture, women's rights, and the many other attempts at change—any observer can see that after all those efforts only a few real changes have been achieved. Positive social change with justice, especially economic justice, at its core is not on the immediate horizon.

There were only 400 or 500 good "free" schools out of the 2,500 – 3,000 new schools and these involved about 3,000 to 5,000 adults and about 20,000 children, a majority of whom were of elementary age. That's a rather small number, pitifully small, on which to base a revolution.

There is also an over-riding, philosophical point to this issue and it is best expressed in the following quotation from George Dennison:

> God save [the alternative schools] from becoming a "Movement." The power of their ideas is that they are basic. They do not deal with class phenomena, but with the nature of growth. As far as I can see, these ideas have no contenders and are bound to prevail. Practical issues are another question and are certainly political. It's hard to imagine a free school advocate calling for more centralization. The whole [idea behind these schools] is certainly on the left, and seems to be intrinsically Populist or Anarchist. But the Anarchist ideal is that politics transforms itself wholly into function. The beauty of the free schools is that they are—*already*—the very image of

Anarchist function. To politicize the free schools is to go backwards, to become rigid, to lose function and gain nothing but rhetoric. Don't act as if you really love each other just because you want to and say you do. Don't call for solidarity except when there is an important issue, because solidarity in the absence of an issue is nothing but party-line conformity. Be various and flexible. Live in the world, not in a handful of issues.[2]

So, what can be done? What can you and I do? We can start with what we can actually do: put our first and most serious commitment with the 30 or 50 or 200 children in each of the innovative schools; then, work with public school reformers, exchange resources, help others start new schools, criticize our own efforts, even federate, as some schools in larger cities have done. It would be the most profound of mistakes to try to weld the schools into a single ideology, as Dennison says so well in the above quotation.

Small scale activities can stimulate other small-scale actions. Then, when more people are involved, larger changes are possible, changes that are from the bottom up and not from the top down and controlled by a small group of people.

Teachers and schools cannot be neutral in the same way that an individual cannot be neutral. They must involve themselves with ideas and activities that deal with the inequalities and brutalities in America—with the class structure, the exploitation of the poor, racism, colonialism, sexism and many other issues like the environment which show that the system is haywire.

Educators can lend themselves to this struggle by being deeply involved as active agents for change within their own schools and, where time and energy permit, by aligning themselves with other people who are working in similar directions, while not losing focus on the children in their classes and schools.

This brings me back to the Stamford Early Learning Center. What I observed there indicates that it is a healthy place for children, but that it can do and be more. As noted, the school serves middle-to-upper class, entitled families; it is not involved with poor children or children of color, and so it reinforces inequalities.

In contrast to this, I can point to the Graham & Parks Alternative Public School (Cambridge, MA) which deliberately set admissions quotas so that the school would be balanced by race, gender and socio-economic backgrounds. It believed that heterogeneous groups of students, staff and parents are the best starting points on which to build learning. Margaret Skutch's school has much to offer us because it truly helps its children to develop curiosity, sharing and cooperation; the children learn how to learn, to discover for themselves; they learn skills and develop as individuals while having a deep sense of caring and respect for others and the like. The school actualizes much of the rhetoric of alternative school people.

But the children grow up with a limited view of reality. They do not interact with a variety of children and they do not see the social realities or the changes that must be made. Just infusing the unit on Native Americans mentioned earlier with a study of how they were cruelly treated would make a good beginning. Raising funds to bring in poor children and children of color—not as tokens—could be a second step for the school to take. Another action could be establishing a similar school in a poor area for the children who live there.

Many years ago, I visited the St. Paul (MN) Open School. A teacher, Joe Nathan, had a group of high school students researching problems in the city, such as pollution, practices of real estate agents in steering people to certain areas and the like. Not only did the students have to research a topic they had chosen, they had to inform the community of their results and they were to come up with solutions that they were to try to implement.

The ideal is to weld the educational process at ELC with socially conscious materials and activities like those just noted, to weld great success in teaching a small group of real children to grow in their own individual ways and success in bringing together children from a wide variety of backgrounds and starting the process of personal change, social awareness and social change. The ideal is to weld the kind of molecular, moral forces that William James talks about with the kind of social force that Jonathan Kozol is talking about. This would give us the best chance of transforming our personal lives, our schools and our society.

Notes

1. Some of these books include George Dennison's *The Lives of Children*, Jonathan Kozol's *Free the Children*, Jim Herndon's *How to Survive in Your Own Land*, *The School in Rose Valley* by Grace Rotzel, Platt's *I Learn From Children* and Len Solo's *Making an Extraordinary School: The Work of Ordinary People*.

2. Letter from George Dennison, *KOA Newsletter*, #2.

Chapter 4
Strawberry Fields Forever?

For a variety of reasons, when some people hear the words "innovative," "charter" and "alternative" schools, they automatically think of good, humane schools where children have fun learning.

I've visited many alternative and innovative schools over the years and I've found that some are really high quality places, while others are just okay, and a few are very weak.

I've also talked with hundreds of educators in these schools over the years. Almost all have been decent, sincere people, many of them deeply concerned about their children and the damage that many traditional public schools are doing to children, good-hearted people who are truly trying to make viable learning places for their children. And they are brave, because to leave the known public schools behind and to voyage into the unknown of starting a new school with little money, constant harassment and not much more than their determination, dreams and good-heartedness demands bravery.

Yet, some people turned to establishing alternative schools in an attempt to solve their own problems. This means that some were exploiting their own children, using their children to create an image of a better world for themselves. Others plunged ahead setting up schools with barely an understanding of the complexities in founding and running a school, while making a really good learning environment was way beyond their conception and or skills.

I could illustrate this with examples from the many alternative schools I have seen firsthand: the high school for drop-outs and push-outs in Vermont where the students either played ping-pong day after day or had spitting-water-on-each-other battles; the rich kids' school west of Boston where the adults would only teach when asked by the children, who didn't seem to ask very often and sat around the kitchen constantly bored; and the urban "free" school run by two hip white teachers who wanted the Black children to be joyful and loving and "to get into all kinds of neat things," while the parents wanted their children to learn to read and do math, while the kids ran wildly around the building hurting each other verbally and physically and destroying any neat project that a child would dare to get into.

I would rather show one, concrete, specific example of an alternative school run by parents who were operating their school more for themselves than for their children. I don't think the parents knew what they doing and they would be horrified at my judgment. But they established the school to regain a sense of potency and control in their lives, to overcome their loneliness, to create a community of shared interest and to create an image of freedom for their children because they themselves had little real freedom or did not know what to do with the freedom they had.

I am presenting this critical chapter for several reasons: Creating a school is a difficult undertaking. People need to be very clear about what they are doing and why they are doing it. Also, examining a failed effort can be helpful, can be a positive guide to knowing what to do, what not to do and what one needs to know to be successful. It can be as helpful as examining what makes a good school work.

I spent a fair number of hours volunteering in the school which I'll call Strawberry Fields Forever.[1] The parents knew me only as a new graduate student who was interested in "new" schools.

The school was located in a small, two-story house at the top of a pleasant suburban-like street. The house was uncared for outside, but inside it was a mess: torn couches with springs hanging out, broken toys and learning materials scattered about, paper and dust under furniture and in corners. The kids obviously did not pick up after themselves and the adults obviously did not insist that they do, nor did they clean up much after their children. The neighbors, "the straights," a few children told me, repeatedly called the police and complained about the noise and the kids running and climbing on an old school bus and the roof of the house.

The school seemed to have no coherence, no unity, no noticeable structures, no place of calm in the eye of the storm. The parents initially decided they wouldn't bring anything into the school or teach any lessons until the kids asked for or wanted something. As one parent explained, "I don't want to put my thing on a child," an expression of self-abdication I've heard many times since. But most of the younger children couldn't read well and they didn't seem to want to do much either, not often asking the parents for anything.

In order for children to become interested and want to learn, the environment has to have materials to learn from or with. The day has to be planned, there have to be projects which are interesting and challenging so that the children want to become involved, want to satisfy their curiosity, want to learn. Also, teachers need to care by carefully preparing the environment and the materials and projects and by knowing each child really well so that *they* know what the child needs to learn. Of course, the school needs to allow and plan for children discovering things on their own. It also helps if the adults in the school are deeply involved with their own lives so that they have lots of experience and knowledge to bring to the children and that they convey an excitement about learning and living.

After being there a few days, I became depressed and stayed at home to think about the school. I decided to re-read some of the education books that I liked, thinking that perhaps I could then see Strawberry Fields Forever from a different perspective. I read all or parts of *Summerhill, I Learn From Children, How Children Fail, Our Children Are Dying, Schools for Tomorrow, The Lives of Children* and Tolstoy and Emerson on education.

I was again infused with the romantic spirit of education. "Romantic" means a certain positive philosophy about people and life—encompassing the rational but, also, embracing the emotional, physical, intuitive, spiritual and holistic—and not foolish, impractical or dreamy. Children want to make sense of the world as they grow up and into it. If they learn what they need and want to help them make the sense they seek, become involved with things which have meaning for them, learn with and from other children, sort of mess with the world, learn at their own pace and in their own time, with the help of adults, they usually learn with comparative ease and success.

What is often taught in many schools is nonsense that we forget easily. I remember sitting in a cafeteria one day and overhearing two girls talking. One asked the other the definition of a word. The second girl couldn't remember it either until the first girl said that it was on the next day's test. Neither girl could recall the word's meaning. The only reason the word was of interest was to pass a test. It had no meaning, no connections, to their real lives. As soon as the test was over, they probably would forget the word and probably acquire a negative attitude toward gaining new ones, at least in school.

The books also helped me to again realize the curiosity and creativity of children and how well they all can learn in their attempts to understand the world, to construct and re-construct it in their minds out of their evolving experiences, their experiences of seeing, touching, hearing, smelling, tasting and doing things in the world. John Holt's example of a child learning to talk is a fine example of this.

After reading the books, I decided to take another look at Strawberry Fields Forever. I still did not think the school was any good for the kids. It did have one positive aspect, though. There was much socializing among the children, so everybody knew each other. Some of the parents taught in the school and they treated each child gently and seemed to give them plenty of love, holding and hugging the children often. The only thing is, and both A. S. Neill and Bruno Bettelheim mention this, love isn't enough. It is important but much more is needed. What is needed is careful teaching.

The same goes for freedom. Freedom is the starting point of a humane education, not the end. Once children have some control over what and how they learn, when they are actively involved in their learning, they need real options to choose from, real help from real people, people who have the skills and knowledge to know what kids need, know how to listen to children and know how to provide for them in appropriate ways, know how to deepen and broaden the child's experiences.

The parents at the school obviously didn't know what or how to teach their children. They had a vague A. S. Neill/Sudbury Valley School concept that freedom was all that was necessary for children to thrive. Take away the constraints of the evil public schools and children would naturally learn was what they thought.

This was the first year for the school, which had about 30 kids, between the ages of four and eight. Two of the parents were the main teachers, though they were not certified and had not taught before. A fair number of the other parents volunteered for several hours a day, so there were enough adults around to supervise the children. These volunteers would sometimes come in with a lesson or activity. At morning meeting, the "schedule" for the day was explained to the kids and the volunteer parents would explain what they were prepared to do with kids that day. But it was up to the kids to choose to participate in the activity. Some did. Those children who did varied from day to day and there was no consistency and little follow-up. There were several field trips each week to museums, zoos, places of business and the like. Most of the kids went on these trips, but, again, they were not well planned and were not part of any on-going studies. So, in this regard, the school functioned a bit like Summerhill.

I went to the school because I wanted to see the start of an alternative school from its beginning. When I arrived a few weeks into the first term, I didn't feel as if I fit in with the school. Parents did not know how to involve me in the teaching-learning process and I spent several days doing little but hanging around and then I'd leave when I got really bored.

A short while later I picked up on Holt's idea and I'd bring an item into school and sit around and do things with it, like using multi-based blocks to teach a few four- and five-year-olds how to count and to add. I did this several days a week, with mostly the same group of kids. I made sandpaper and felt letters and began regularly teaching some kids the alphabet and letter and sound correspondence. Some days I brought in my computer and typed or did research. I found that by doing this the kids would come in and want to know what I was doing. After I explained or showed them, they would want to try for themselves. Another time, I bought a stack of magazine and started making a collage. I think most of the kids made collages that day!

I brought in children's books and, at first, would sit and read one to myself until a few kids joined me. Then, I'd read it to them, holding it so they could see the drawings. I asked them questions about the book, about the characters, the plot, the ideas, pointing out words and letters, doing this in a casual, seemingly off-handed way, even asking kids to write something about the books.

A number of alternative school teachers make a simple

doctrine of total child freedom and choice. But kids don't learn that way. They especially do not learn the things they need to make their way in this world, so teachers cannot function in one way. At points in their days, children need freedom; at other points, they need to be taught by knowledgeable adults. There are all sorts of rhythms and cycles between these two points in a child's learning and an adult's teaching. Teaching involves relationships with children that go from authoritarian on a continuum all the way left to discovery and choice. A true teacher functions along this entire continuum from being a giver of commands, to a task guider, to one who designs individual programs, to one who facilitates discovery, to one who lets children learn on their own.

The two parent teachers saw what I was doing. So, I began talking with them about what I was doing and what I thought they could be doing and how the school could be run. It was like conducting a course in Teaching 101 because I had to go back and explain that a school should have various structures like defined areas for doing certain learning activities—a science area with appropriate materials, an area for math stocked with math materials, a reading and writing area with books, papers and writing materials, an arts area with paint, easels, crayons, pencils and various kinds of paper—like a house with a kitchen, a bathroom and a bedroom.

In this world, kids have to learn to read and to write, to do math, know science, history, art and the like. They have to learn these to a high level. They also have to learn how to learn.

The best way for kids to learn is to get them actively involved in their own learning by using materials, doing hands-on activities and by doing projects that teachers develop, with input from the students. Kids can learn a great deal with and from each other, so the school also needs to organize itself to facilitate this happening.

Above all, teachers must be the ones to arrange this environment and develop the structures for the children. They need to provide consistency in how they teach reading and math on a daily basis and how they provide the children with opportunities to be involved and to help choose what they do.

This was not easy for me to do because I had been a high school teacher and, at that point, had not worked very much with younger children in schools. I gave the teachers practical books to read on how to teach reading, math and science and how to use learning centers in open classrooms. I did some modeling of lessons and provided feedback to their efforts. I helped them develop groups and schedules for these groups.

But I could not be there every day. I had my own studies and projects to do for my graduate work, I had a family that needed me and the school was not paying me. The school got better and better as the year progressed but I had to withdraw from the school when some personal issues came up that I had to attend to with some urgency.

The improvement was not enough. By the end of the year, most of the parents realized the school was a failure. Some had withdrawn their children, a few were planning to move and some of the children wanted to go back to their neighborhood public school. Some parents asked me to run the school, but I declined. At a contentious meeting in May, the parents decided to not re-open the school.

Strawberry Fields Forever may sound like a caricature, but it was a real school where some real children were failed.

Some "new" schools failed for various reasons: lack of money; failure to teach basic skills; failure to achieve strong adult leadership; failure to develop fully the founding ideals; failure to see that freedom involves responsibility and discipline; failure to provide on-going, humane, individualized learning; failure to provide choices for students, choices buttressed with materials and plans; failure to develop a community; external pressures by local public school administrators, neighbors and health, fire and building inspectors; profound philosophical rifts; and some schools that go well for a time die because the teachers involved burn themselves out from the vast amount of work that is necessary to run a truly child-centered school. Teaching, especially teaching young children, is very hard work.

There *are* many good alternative, innovative schools that have continued to grow and thrive in almost every section of the country. I described one in the previous chapter. More are shown in books like *To Start a School, Raspberry Exercises, The Making of an Extraordinary School, Summerhill, The School in Rose Valley, Spearpoint, Crisis in the Classroom, Free the Children, Free Schools* and Deborah Meier's *In Schools We Trust* and *The Power of Their Ideas*. Some good schools are shown in films like *Play Mountain Place, Summerhill, The Everdale Place, Sometimes I Even Like Me, What's New at School*, and *Children as People*. In Lennon and McCartney's words, these are "places you can go where everything flows." Given a good alternative school, I would choose it over anything else.

Later, I became the principal of one of these very good schools—the Graham & Parks Alternative Public School in Cambridge, MA. Strawberry Fields Forever provided solid, negative lessons for me that I put to use almost every day at Graham & Parks. We established a large number of carefully designed structures that were the bases for the school's success. (*Redbook* magazine dubbed it "one of the country's outstanding schools" and it was the Disney Spotlight School of the Year 2000.) Some of these included: parent involvement supported by a full-time Parent Coordinator; staff development supported by a full-time Staff Developer; parents shared equally with staff in all decision-making through a variety of committees that included a Steering Committee, hiring, evaluation, social, curriculum and the like; a set of beliefs and practices that all ascribed to with a passion; classes were structured as self-contained, multi-graded, open classrooms at K-6, with a student-centered 7-8 program; all teachers worked on vertical and horizontal teams which met weekly, if not daily, to plan, share and learn together; and children were admitted by lottery in categories of race, social class and gender so that the school was well balanced. In other words, we planned carefully all aspects of the school's functioning.

In *The Aims of Education*, Alfred Lord Whitehead discusses three stages of learning that we go through in the process of solving a problem. First is the Romance stage, when a person perceives new connections, has a vision of a changed future, and commits to exploring and understanding these connections. The second stage is Precision, when a person masters the tools of inquiry of a discipline and fleshes out the details of his/her initial insights and perceptions. The third stage is Generalization, when a person stands up from his desk and confidently adventures into the world with the power of bodies of organized insight, implementing and constantly expanding her/his vision.

Whitehead's metaphors are valuable for understanding the alternative and innovative schools of the 1960s and 1970s. Their early years can be seen as the Romance Stage when people perceived that the child must be the center of education (and not the teacher, the curriculum or the school) and they started doing battle with the evil giants (and pygmies) of public education, literally questioning every aspect of what went on in traditional classrooms and schools and trying out all sorts of new ideas from multi-age grouping to schools that had no building but conducted their learning in the community. It was a time of rapid growth and exhilaration in breaking free of past bonds and voyaging into new lands.

But the growth leveled off and some of the older schools moved into the Precision Stage—while the rest of the counter culture slipped quietly away into more drugs, into the California and Vermont hills, into business suits or into totally hip, freaky and irrelevant activities.

The concerns of people in this stage were with curricula, with materials, with school structures and with figuring out how people relate to each other, especially the children, around these materials, projects and curricula. They went back to John Dewey's emphasis on *the child **and** the curriculum*.

During that time, I visited a class in an alternative school during Chanukah, a holiday of freedom, when the teachers and children were in the process of lighting the candles in the menorah. As it was lit, a candle was dedicated to a revolutionary figure—Tom Paine, Simon Bolivar, Dr. Martin Luther King, Cesar Chavez and the like. Prior to this day, children choose a person they wanted to study, which they did. Then, a child presented his person to the rest of the class as a candle was being lit. The children participated in a religious ceremony, learned about a religion (most were not Jews) and learned fantastic "social studies" lessons. This teacher, actually this school, was in the Precision Stage where the concern was with mastering the tools of one's trade, with teachers getting really good at choosing what to teach and how to teach it well.

A little later, I visited a progressive school which was established in 1928. One reason that it has survived is the way learning is organized. Study in classes is structured around units, ideas and themes of interest to the students and the teachers. For example, one second grade teacher had gotten excited about bees and his excitement sparked his class. The kids made large bees (2 feet long, but with no stingers the children had decided) which hung from the ceiling or were set in a cardboard hive that covered one wall. Books about bees were read; the kids saw movies and slide presentations about bees; the class visited a beekeeper and his hives; the children had painted a mural of bees, flowers, trees and sky over one entire wall; and three children were writing a bee play which was to be performed by the class for the entire school, parents included. The excitement in the room was obvious. Here was an inter-disciplinary curriculum which had the children actively involved in art, math, construction, field trips, multi-media, reading, writing, drama and sharing.

This class exemplified Whitehead's Generalization Stage, where the teacher has complete understanding and control of his materials, understands how to get children involved and excited about learning and is boldly confident in his work with children, confident about high quality work.

In the above examples, the teachers are truly freeing the children to learn by their careful construction of lessons and activities. During the 1960s and 1970s, there was much prattle and unclear thinking among school people about freedom. One wrote me, quoting a song by Janis Joplin, to say "Freedom's just another word for nothing left to lose." This is the concept that freedom is a process of shedding, a shucking of constraints, like a snake in the spring which sheds the skin it's outgrown. In part, this is what freedom involves, the slaves cutting their chains, the James Joyce's breaking the nets that bind them to home, religion and country, and the teacher getting rid of the desks in rows and setting up learning centers in her room. But, for me, freedom is also involved in a statement that Nietzsche once made: "The artist is he who dances in chains." The painter is constrained by the flat canvas yet she can make curves, round objects and have depth, can create a real-looking world in a small space—thus dancing in her chains.

We are all chained in a variety of ways—by our bodies, by our minds, by our emotions, by our past, by our family, by our friends, by our possessions, by our country, etc. The free person is the one who takes the bonds and learns to control them and use them so s/he can dance. It is impossible to never have chains, but we can *release* ourselves through the chains.

For me, freedom is nothing more than nor less than the space that is generated around the lives of free people. And a free person is one who is making the best uses she knows how to of all her capacities, initiating change, moving forward into activities, constantly improving. That is the point about the above two examples from the schools I'd visited. There, free adults were helping children to become free.

Freedom means planning, hard work, development of curricula, teaching strategies, projects, making materials and working hard at human relationships. It's the Precision Stage that one must master *before* adventuring into the world with our children so we do not get lost like the parents in Strawberry Fields Forever.

Notes

1. This is my name for the school, from Lennon and McCartney's "Glass Onion." It's a song that could be used as an anthem for some of the new schools:

> I told you about Strawberry Fields
> You know the place where nothing is real
> Well, here's another place you can go
> Where everything flows...

Chapter 5
New School Curriculum Report

I founded the Atlantic County New School in 1972. Initially, the school was located in Atlantic City and then it moved to a nearby town. We had about 40 children, ages 5-13, divided into two groups. It was run as a parent cooperative and had children from a wide variety of economic, social and racial backgrounds. This report was written in 1974 by the school's two main teachers, Manya Bean and Joan Hink, with some input from me.

This year we've again tried to create a curriculum as diverse as possible in terms of content and in terms of people. We consider ourselves primarily responsible for teaching the three R's and for seeing to it that the children grow and are happy. We have a lot of related tasks and we do them according to our capabilities, talents and energy levels. Nevertheless, for the study of separate disciplines and for our many and diverse activities, including field trips and flea markets, we depend on outside help.

We structure our days, then, around those activities that relate to our responsibilities and those that are carried out by other people in the form of workshops. You will read here a list of materials that we have chosen to use in teaching the three

R's and a description of all the workshops and the people who have enriched our days these past ten months.

Our days are a combination of structure and choice, a concern for children and for their curriculum and how these inter-connect. The mornings are usually devoted to skill development and other academic work: reading, writing, math, science, etc., with specific times set aside for each activity. We work with each child. We start with where each child is at, but we do not leave him/her there: we work with individuals, small groups and, sometimes, the entire group.

After lunch, we have workshops—ones that utilize the skills of our high school volunteers, our three senior citizens, our many college practicum students, some college faculty and our parents. We also make many trips in the afternoons: to the nearby wildlife refuge, to the local state college, to the ocean, to Philadelphia, to local businesses, to historical sites, or we go on environmental science walks.

On Fridays, students leave at 1:30 and we have parent conferences from then until 4:30.

For language arts, we use our own phonics program, Gattegno's *Words in Color* Program, the *Bank Street Readers* and a series of phonic "comic books" from Scholastic. We also use the organic reading approach as described by Sylvia Ashton-Warner in *Teacher* and *Spearpoint*. For 4th, 5th and 6th grades, we have a series of texts that are not written necessarily for children but are anthologies of interesting writings by interesting people. For 7th grade, we have a literature program from Scholastic, but we need more materials for 7th and 8th graders. We also have writing books for all levels and an interesting assortment of materials in the form of recipe cards from the California Creative Press. We have some books from McDonald's Publishing House in England and we are constantly looking for more materials for all levels.

This is, of course, bare bones. We use many of the activities in Ken Koch's *Wishes, Lies and Dreams*, Gordon and Poze's

Strange and Familiar, Sandy Fluck's *Experiential English*, James Moffett's *A Student-Centered Language Arts Curriculum, K-13*, Herb Kohl's *Writing, Math and Games in the Open Classroom* and many more such practical resources.

A great deal goes on with written and spoken language, from captions for paintings and photographs to homemade books; from graffiti walls and the copying of recipes to serious reports and responsible journalism; from writing letters and messages to each other to Haiku poems; from composing language while listening to someone improvise on the flute to listening to a Langston Hughes poem read by Ossie Davis and copying it down; to conspiring on the creation of an underground sheet as opposed to the "Junior Journal" and so on almost *ad infinitum*.

The books for arithmetic are the following: 1) *Math Workshop*, Levels O-E, from Encyclopedia Britannica. These books, according to Ralph Bean, head of the Math Program at Stockton State College, "are particularly well suited because they base the learning of the algorithms on the natural desire to find short cuts to the answers of problems. In addition, they are suited to our style of teaching." 2) *Stretches and Shrinkers*, "because they teach fractions and decimals in a non-painful way." 3) *Geometry – Fun with Fundamentals*, "because kids like them." We have ordered *You + Math = Fun*, a series of books of word problems and the Nuffield Math Program from England for next year.

Again, these are only books. Ralph Bean has only been able to work individually with some of the older children this year. However, we had two full-time student teachers majoring in Math and Sue Haynie worked almost full-time in the Fall with the younger group using multi-based Dienes blocks in a most effective manner. There is a mini-Math Lab in the older students' room which utilizes tanagrams, soma cubes, problem sheets, puzzles and games, many home-made. The lab is designed to foster logical thinking and stimulate creative problem-solving. We would like to add to what we have, order more manipulative materials for all of the children and include scales and measuring devices.

Our Arts program is phenomenal. If our resident artist-parent of last year, Margaret Haggerty, were here, she would thoroughly approve because no day passes by without someone making something. The materials the children have used include poster and finger paints, water colors, charcoal, colored chalk, many different textured clays, both commercial and home-made. They have been involved in printing with various materials, in silk-screening, in batik, collages and cardboard sculptures. Margo Achille, our Art student teacher, has been an inspiration. She and the children have used plaster of Paris in an amazing number of ways. The crafts have included weaving on Inkle looms, cardboard looms and weaving between twigs and branches. In our candle-making, we again used a great variety of molds from paper cups and tin cans to sand molds and sea shells. We've done macramé, puppets, decoupage, beading, bridge books, cartoons, a lot of sewing and needle-work, and we'll stop.

Finally, we prefer that Social Studies be seen as an integral part of the curriculum—meaning our everyday life with each other, rather than a separate workshop or study unit. When we happen to have a student teacher who happens to be a 35 year-old Black ex-cop, and when we just happen to have seen a film called "What It Means to Be a Black Policeman," it is appropriate that we sit down with him and discuss police work, the law, the uses of weapons, visit his old police station and the like. When a new child uses racist language because he hasn't learned better yet, we have a "lesson" on racism, on racial and ethnic minorities in this country and on the percentage of people of color around the world. We study Native Americans by having Lorraine Gormley and Chris McGaffney show us their slides of their two months in Wounded Knee, South Dakota. Then, we go to Stockton State College and talk with

Native Americans who are visiting a class and who are guests of the college. We eat their food and join in their dance. We deal with political action or inaction, with power and powerlessness, with children's and people's rights when we hear Jonathan Kozol at the college and then speak with him afterwards. There is no better way to learn about oppression than by experiencing our own oppression in our quest for a home for our school. We deal with sex and age chauvinism as it comes up every day in our lives. Most importantly, we try to learn about community, about caring for each other, having control over our lives, by building our school together, by caring and giving ourselves choices.

Next year, we're thinking we may use some of the *Man: A Course of Study* materials and some of the social studies materials developed by Sources.

Our workshops have been really successful this year. It is possible that we were more ready for them this year than last. Here is a list of our favorites: Our most remarkable Kathy Krajewski, college student and dear friend, with the help of Libby Marsh, Stockton professor, conducted a most effective geography workshop during the fall term. It included studying and researching in libraries, the writing of reports, field trips, and sessions at Stockton with Libby and her fantastic maps.

John Wessler, another student teacher, led a workshop in the Winter term which included dissection of a frozen squirrel and a cardinal, both victims of car accidents, and of fish. The students made diagrams of the dissections, set up a fish tanks, brine shrimp tanks and gerbil cages. Students learned to keep daily logs of these creatures. There were daily discussions about the creatures as well as reading of books about vertebrates, Petri plates, compost piles, looking through microscopes and the like. John, even though he completed his requirements at the end of the winter term, continued to come every week until the end of the school year.

Ruth Yarrow, Stockton professor, and a group of her

students chose to work with us during the fall and winter terms in an environmental studies program. This workshop consisted of a series of field trips with a session preparing us for the trip as well as a follow-up session. Each session and each trip was an exciting and productive event. One college student, Bill Haas, then continued these activities through the spring term.

Several trips to Stockton at the invitation of Sandy Hartzog, parent and faculty member, were for the older group a fortunate continuation of the environmental workshop. Her sessions in the science lab, outdoors and in the greenhouse were just what we needed. The herbs and plants our children started with her are now growing at the school and in the children's homes.

We try to plan carefully for the school year. Yet, a number of the good things that happen at the New School are the result of what we call "a happy accident." Perhaps our proximity to so many talented and gifted parents and other resource people, especially at the college, coupled with our flexibility and readiness to use what is in front of us, result in good happenings. Things often somehow work out, mesh together, and suddenly there appears the creation of a good whole out of the merging of the planning and the happy accidents.

The two main teachers and several students have been regularly leading workshops in creative writing and poetry. We also do role-playing and Gestalt games and exercises.

Linda Nesbitt's (a retired editor) newspaper workshop has for two years been one of our more nourishing staples.

Charlie Marsh, retired engineer and teacher, worked with us again this year. He conducted workshops in thermodynamics and on solar heating, and he invited us to his darkroom to develop and print our pictures. We also had a session with him where we learned that what happens in the darkroom "ain't just magic."

Our physical education program picked up this spring with the advent of the GREAT TED JONES, Stockton student and athlete. He and the children measured out a 150 meter course and a 450 meter one. They all ran against the clock. He also taught wrestling and boxing, soccer and baseball. He kept a beautiful journal of all the activities and everyone is invited to look in and read it.

Valerie Plazzo, a drama student, has worked in the New School for two terms. She did drama exercises and improvisations and then directed and produced a play with the children as part of her senior project. The children are very creative in this area, especially our younger children, where we daily see puppet shows, skits and spontaneous role playing.

Our music program has had some gaps, especially in comparison to last year when we had the help of a fine student teacher. Don Haynie worked with us in the fall and Lorraine Gormley in the spring. Their work culminated with our entire school's singing debut at the college.

Our children did a great deal of cooking and baking, planting seeds and nurturing plants, woodworking and building.

A lot happened.

The previous section was about people and their workshops. This section is special. It is important to us that our children come in contact with people of all ages and backgrounds. So, there are a number of high school people from Holy Spirit who come to us two afternoons a week and function as interns. Mary and Lisa in particular have contributed much to all of us. Then, we have our senior citizens. Three people—Helen, Florence and Fred—have come every Monday throughout the year. They've cooked, they've sewed, they read stories, they played games, they went to the store and they shared a great deal. On Monday, Florence was there, being her usual fine self, and on Thursday we learned that she had died. It was very hard for us to say good-by.

Many parents worked in and for the school: teaching,

reading, setting up trips, driving us around, making materials, cleaning the rooms, and attending the bi-monthly meetings.

All of this happened, we should finally note, on a total budget that is less than a quarter of what a public education costs.

Len Solo
from philip

Chapter 6
One of You Is Sufficient

Once, the story goes, while Ralph Waldo Emerson was visiting a school, a teacher invited him to observe her class. She ran her students through their usual paces: she had them do math drills, read aloud, do grammar and the like. After school was over, she asked Emerson what he thought about the class. He replied: "Madam, I perceive that you are trying to make all of these children just like you. One of you is sufficient."

I've thought about this Emerson incident because I've been thinking a great deal about my father and how much he is a part of me. I've been thinking about the father in me.

When I joked with my two sons and slowly intoned, "No, no, no, my boys, don't give me any of that bull," I'd see my father in my head and hear him say that to me in the same tone, wagging a finger in front of my nose. I'd bend over to pick a toy off the floor and images of my father bending over to pick up things flashed behind my eyes, my body bent like his, one arm reaching and the other stiff at my side as if it's paralyzed.

I'd let my children take turns "driving" the car when we were near home. Lenny or Chris would sit on my lap and I'd hold them with the left hand and with the finger-tips of the right hand I'd gently touch the steering wheel and guide it just like my father did to me when I was six and sat on his knee and thought I was driving his Plymouth coupe.

Even though we were poor, my father told me constantly as I grew up that I would go to college. He held the egalitarian notion that anyone's child who is capable should be able to attend college. My father's ambition was for me to be someone he wasn't, to achieve what he did not achieve, for me to not be a coal miner, a farmer, a carpenter or a factory worker, but to want to go to college. I did.

My father is in me more deeply than that. He could not easily accept or give affection and I see that this is in me, too, like an inner layer of an onion that takes much peeling before it is reached and touched.

My father, then, is in me, in the inner recesses of my skull and in all the cells of my blood. When I think of this, I realize Emerson's words: "I perceive that you are trying to make all of these children just like you. One of you is sufficient." And I think of my own children and the children of other parents: what do we do to our children? How are people formed? By whom? How are we putting ourselves into our children? For what purposes? Is this good?

When my son, Chris, was young, he'd do things quickly and it was not easy for my other son, Lenny, to give affection. I see myself and my father in them. I, too, wanted them to go to college, wanted them to get to a better place beyond me.

Is this what all fathers want for their children? When my kids were younger, I didn't think much about this, but I had a vague feeling that I wanted them to have a chance to do more with their lives than I had, to go beyond the limits that came from growing up as I had. I had a desire for Lenny and Chris to grow up and be happy, to get a good education, to get a good job and not suffer or hurt other people. I wanted them to be "good" kids and to grow up to be "good" adults.

I, also, wanted them to be different, to be individuals who saw themselves as equals with any and everyone, to be on the side of the liberals, the good guys, to be concerned with their rights and the rights of others, to be passionate about justice.

I wanted them to mirror what I saw in myself, though I never said this to them directly.

It's important to see how parents' attitudes toward their children effect how our schools function. If we want our children to have roomy houses on two-acre, suburban lots, with a pretty wife and two children inside and two trendy cars in the garage, then we're telling the schools: Look, make sure my kid is in the upper 20% of her class, make sure she's a red bird and not a blue bird, make sure she's a winner (or places or shows, but is not one of the pack in this race), make sure she's concerned primarily with herself, make sure you have a somewhat pleasant school where she feels pretty good about herself, where you let her have some freedom but still push her hard and still have her walk in lines and raise her hand, let her play with gerbils, listen to tapes of individualized grammar lessons or stories by Dr. Seuss, or play with the Cuisenaire rods, but don't let her get too excited about anything, too passionate about poverty, racism, sexism or social class abuse, so passionate that it will lead her to action. Don't disturb her sleep.

Have others decide what and how she'll learn. Teach her to be mostly passive, though you can let her talk quietly in cooperative learning groups, so she'll be a person who willingly watches a lot of television, who will buy and own a lot of things and will dress according to the fashion of the season.

But what if the goals for our children were different? How would this change our schools? What if we set our sights on having children grow up to be like our heroes and heroines, not happy, well-adjusted citizens, but good people—*good* people like Dr. Martin Luther King, Thoreau, Gandhi, Tolstoy, St. Joan, Malcolm X, Chavez, Dolci, Helen Keller, Septima Clark, Myles Horton, Helen Keller and Mother Jones—good people who strive to live their lives all the way up, who believe that the best way to live is for others and not for narrow and closed self-interest, to live ethical lives based on justice, truth and community?

In the early '70s I was in charge of a small teacher preparation program which I had designed in a new state college near Atlantic City and so I had a chance to often visit the local public schools to see what was going on in classrooms. The innovation that was sweeping the area was the Learning Center Approach to teaching. In such classrooms, there are anywhere from five to eight learning stations in various parts of the room: Listening Center, Reading Center, Math Center, Science Center, Art Center and the like—where students are programmed to do specific "discovery" activities. The class is usually divided into four or five homogeneous groups with four or five students in each group. The groups move, in a pre-arranged manner, from one station to another at regular intervals during the day on the teacher's signal, like trains being switched from track to track by an engineer.

The idea behind this approach is to give children more variety, more freedom, give them more choices, have them work with others, let them move more at their own paces and make learning more fun.

I visited a school with learning centers and I remember one room, particularly one center in that classroom. It was a bright, cheery center that was concerned with blueberries. *BLUEBERRIES* was spelled out in large letters across the top of a two-paneled, folding screen about four feet high. The screen was covered with a bright contact paper and it had colorful pictures of berries on it, workers picking them in a field, pictures of berries being processed in a factory, being sold in a grocery store and at a roadside stand and of blueberries being eaten in cereal by a smiling family of four.

I asked the teacher how the center worked. She showed me packets of numbered questions attached to the screen. The kids had to find answers to the questions like some of the following: Where are the blueberries primarily grown? What is their nutritional value? Weigh a berry and then determine how many berries are in a pound. What's the cost of one berry?

Look at the pictures in this learning center and write a story using one of them.

"That's pretty good," I told the teacher. "The kids get into health and nutrition, do research work, write and use math with this learning station. The berries are grown here in South Jersey and I guess you use this to get them into local history?"

"Yes, I've made up some questions about that," she responded, showing me the packet of questions that she was referring to.

"Do you have any questions that get these kids angry over these blueberries?"

She smiled. "What do you mean, get them angry? Over blueberries?"

"Well, these berries are picked by migrant workers, aren't they? Do you ask your students to find out how much money migrant workers earn a year? Do you investigate the migrants' working conditions? Do you research who profits from these workers? Do you have the kids figure out which politicians have allowed this to happen for the past fifty years?"

"No!" She got angry. "What are you talking about? These children are too young for stuff like that!"

If she hadn't left, I would have asked how old they would have to be to learn that these migrants are almost all Black or Spanish-speaking and earn less that $4,000 a year, that some of the parents of the children in this classroom may even be owners of large berry enterprises and benefited directly from this slave labor and that these children should be told about their parents' deeds? When would they be old enough to read the following from the April 1969 pages of the *New York Times*?

> At one farm [in New Jersey, Blacks] have been crowded into chicken coops. In another, they cook, drink and bathe from a foul water tap that has been grossly polluted by a nearby privy... In every camp,

flies swarm over the garbage-strewn dust, the young children, the cooking grits and vegetables that migrants usually live on.

At night in the camps as many as six or more children are stacked like cordwood onto one roach-infested bed... Many children have distended navels, indicating malnutrition, and many also are ridden with lice and ticks. Worm-infested infants, left unattended in camps for hours by their mothers in the fields, are sometimes bitten by rats.

Would the children in this "neat" classroom have to wait until they went through six or seven more years of blueberry learning stations before they were faced with such questions, old enough to be well-educated, well-indoctrinated, well-fed, emotions etherized, ethics dimmed, old enough to help their parents run the blueberry operation, or to go to the store and buy berries cheaply and smile at the bargain, not thinking about their connections to the migrants who picked the berries? Then, could we ask them the questions and expect them to act?

I may have been too hard on this teacher, may have even been placing my beliefs onto a teacher who had developed a good learning center on blueberries; but that learning center was neutral, was limited in that it was safe with "nice" questions, not questions that excite people to passionate, ethical actions, asks the kind of questions that lead people to justice, to helping other people, that lead to developing *good* people.

I taught some of the older brothers and sisters of the children in that blueberry classroom. After I returned from the visit I just described, I asked these men and women in my college class a series of questions: what is the racial make-up of people in Atlantic City? (The college is in the rural pine barrens about 15 miles west of the city.) All got this right: mostly Black and Puerto Rican. What is the racial make-up of Brigantine, Margate, Ventnor, Absecon, Northfield and Linwood, the island and mainland communities around Atlantic City? Right, again: mostly white.

"What's the connection here?" I asked. No one wanted to answer. But I continued.

"What's the average income of people in Atlantic City?" No one knew that it was less than $4,000 a year, though a few suspected it was low. (This is pre-casino Atlantic City.)

"What's the average income of people on the other islands and mainland communities?" Correct: over $15,000 a year.

"What's the connection here?" I asked again. No one knew! These students are between 18 and 24 years old and they did not know about exploitation, social class, and racism in their backyards, did not see the connections.

I tried to get them to think about it. "Why are there no industries in Atlantic County, nothing but the resorts and beaches and farming?" Ah, ha! One student saw the connection, saw that the resort businesses and farms needed cheap labor and so they kept out any other industries. This student even remembered that a few years before—just when janitors, bell-hops, cleaning women, maids and the like were beginning to organize—young Irish women were brought in to work at wages even lower than what the Blacks and Puerto Ricans received.

I asked some more questions, questions that hit closer to home: Why is the non-white population so small at this four-year college? Why is the college located 15 miles away from Atlantic City, the major population center, and why isn't there bus service to the college from the city? Some responded, but no real connections, so I asked some more questions. What's the racial make-up of students at the local community college?

No answers. No answers to basic questions. Most of these students had lived all their lives in this area, had gone to schools here for over 12 years and none had been confronted with these questions, questions that deal with basic realities, questions that should lead them to anger and indignation, lead them to action to correct these injustices.

But these questions were never raised. The questions are still not being raised now with their younger brothers and sisters in their bright and cheery Learning Centers, centers designed to make learning fun, but not made to raise important issues.

How many schools—especially the schools that see themselves as "open," "innovative," "child-centered," and "humanistic"—how many such schools have learning centers or curriculum with these kinds of questions? Not many, I suspect. I suspect that there are thousands of learning centers like the blueberry one, though.

Another innovation that is spreading around the country is the open classroom. What are open classrooms all about? Recently, while reading Joy Taylor's *Organizing the Open Classroom*, I came upon a partial, twisted answer contained in the following paragraph:

> We are not here concerned with broad philosophical aims, but with the practical objectives of good class organization which already have been summarized: the happiness and well-being of every child and his progress according to his capacity; the encouragement of initiative and self-reliance in an atmosphere of controlled freedom; and the individual approach in teaching that modern practice requires. The supporters of the Integrated Day believe that these objectives are more readily attained if both children and teachers are free to follow a less centrally directed programme, or, more accurately, a programme in which central direction is less evident.

Is this what some open classrooms are about? Is this how a non-conventional idea is being perverted by established educators? A more subtle form of indoctrination? A brave new world of the present in which freedom is equated with less evident central direction? For what world of unfreedom would Joy Taylor have us indoctrinate our children?

I think about this: think about all those forces that maintain the status quo—Ford Foundation, I.B.M., Carnegie Corporation, Westinghouse, U. S. Department of Education, Xerox, most colleges of education, state departments of education and on and on—who are now on the open classroom bandwagon, many producing materials and consultants for use in developing open classrooms.

Are these agencies really for producing self-reliant people, self-reliant as Thoreau, Chavez, Dr. King and Gandhi? Are we on the brink of the glorious revolution where the forces of social control, class control, economic control and political control are willing to support, sanction and subsidize their own destruction?

None of these corporations make materials that are not neutral and none manufacture learning stations or individualized materials that are calculated to make students go to the mountains like Dr. King, Mao or Che, or to Walden like Thoreau, or to sainthood like St. Joan, or to socialism like Helen Keller or to civil disobedience like Gandhi.

As a matter of fact, they often make materials that are false. Our social studies texts teach us how the Pan-American Highway was the way the U.S. opened up travel between us and our Latin American brothers and sisters, a road that led us to become "Good Neighbors." Do any of the individualized materials from I.B.M., Xerox, Westinghouse or Singer tell us that the road was really used by American businesses and government to exploit our South American neighbors? It would be fairly easy to find hundreds of such examples.

The discussion of freedom in learning centers and open classrooms reminds me of a passage from A. S. Neill's *Summerhill*:

> This notion that unless a child is learning something the child is wasting his time is nothing less than a curse—a curse that blinds thousands of teachers... Fifty years ago the watchword was "Learn through doing." Today the watchword is "Learn through playing." Play is thus used only as a means to an end, but to what good end I do not really know.

Play is a child's work—isn't that what some progressive educators say? Play—for what good end, indeed? To better con kids into learning all the things we had trouble teaching in the old, traditional way, the hidden curriculum the kids in the '60s revolted against? Play—so that kids could grow up to be more passionate, more full, more ethical humans? But does anyone really believe that politicians and any of the big companies making educational materials really want schools to grow thousands of people like Helen Keller, Myles Horton and Malcolm X? Freedom and economic justice, in Paul Goodman's words, are still missed revolutions, battles yet to be won, battles that are not being waged on the carpeted floors of most open classrooms around learning centers, gerbil cages and dress-up corners, just as they aren't being fought in traditional classrooms. Freedom is never given; it has to be won.

Parents cannot help influencing their sons and daughters, teachers their students. That was the major point that I began this essay with. But we can help how we influence them.

The questions I asked in my college classroom were not useless. One student began to organize a boycott against a local supermarket which did not sell lettuce picked by Chavez's union. She also planned to organize a fast, a way to show her concern and a way to begin to organize people to help migrant workers in South Jersey, in a state that had the third largest migrant population in the country. Several others in the class eventually joined her.

My children attended an alternative school that I started.

Children in the school also joined in this effort to help migrant workers in our area. They wrote to the Mayor, our state representatives, and the governor. They made signs for those who picketed the local supermarkets. The older children joined their parents on weekend rallies. The children also tried contacting local public school children to see if they could get them involved.

If Emerson walked into this school or into my college classroom, would he say we were trying to make these children just like us, that we parents and teachers were making our children in our own images? Yes. By our actions, we *are* influencing our children and students. We know this. We clearly tell the students that we are doing this. We believe that our influence will help them to grow up to be concerned about their own freedom—the way Thoreau was—and about other people's freedom—like Gandhi. We believe that our children will be less concerned about their own narrow, self-interest—like most Americans—and that they will be concerned about ethical and moral issues—like Dr. King, Septima Clark and Rosa Parks.

Also, we knew that our children will not grow up to be exactly like us, just as we are not exactly like our parents and teachers. I have a friend whose father talked about telling his bosses off. My friend got fired from two teaching jobs because he had to teach in certain ways, ways that his supervisor, department chairperson and principal did not like but which he would not abandon because he know they were good for his students. My son, Chris, is able to give and accept love much more than I, while I know that I give an accept love more than my father.

That's how humanity is: we cannot cut ourselves off from the past or be born full-blown. We have roots, one generation carrying the previous generation inside of ourselves, actually carrying all previous generations inside of ourselves. Yet we are more than our past.

By confronting that past in the continuous process of inquiry and action and the force of our wills, we can change and alter that past.

As parents and teachers, we have a choice: To influence our children narrowly, to have them grow up believing that life and truth are televisionary or to have them grow up to live deep, passionate lives, lives built on justice, to have them grow up to be individuals capable of thoughtful action.

Chapter 7
Community and Education

We are witnessing a profound loss of community in the United States. Evidence of this loss, accelerated from a trend in the early 1960s, has become a major feature of life in the early years of the 21st century. Loss of community is seen everywhere: the increase of people living and working in ghettoized groups; the rise in intolerance of groups toward each other; the number of homeless people; the number of people in jail; the number of children living in poverty; the physical and verbal abuse everywhere; townspeople, even neighbors, not caring for or even knowing each other; the litter on the roads and streets; and the sense of loneliness and isolation felt by many. Our increasing pluralism, the depersonalization of experience, the sense of individual powerlessness, intense specialization and the hyperactive organizing of interest groups are part of the root causes of this fragmentation.

Community is an amorphous word whose meaning often varies greatly. For me, its meaning is best explained in the following "working definition" from Fred Oliver and Donald Newman. A community is a group:

> (1) in which membership is valued as an end in itself, not merely as a means to other ends;

(2) that concerns itself with many and significant aspects of the lives of its members;
(3) that allows competing factions;
(4) whose members share commitment to a common purpose and to procedures for handling conflict within the group;
(5) whose members share responsibility for the actions of the group;
(6) whose members have enduring and personal contact with each other.[1]

In 1971, I sent a questionnaire out to several hundred public and private schools listed as alternative and innovative by a number of groups across the country. Approximately 160 schools returned the study. One of the questions I asked them was a large, general and open-ended one: "How do you directly and consciously strive for community—for belonging, togetherness and sharing?"

The responses form a continuum from schools that did not even understand the concept to places that say they live-work-share-play-plan everything together. I've divided this continuum into the following categories:

1. Not Striving for Community

This category includes schools where relationships among people are rather traditional, where roles are narrowly defined and where getting together is a rather formalized affair. Concord High School and Union High School quoted below are typical examples of schools in this category.

2. Half-Way Houses

This group includes schools that realize the need for community and are striving for it. But, because of various limitations—9:00 to 3:00 schedules, environment, personal inabilities and the like—they are only half-way or part-way toward community. These schools may involve participants in some of the decision-making, grant staff some freedom and responsibility, have community meetings and have some close student-staff relationships; but they have a strong stress on curriculum above all else. So, they are houses and, as the old joke goes, a house is not a home. The Cambridge Pilot Project, the Clinton Program and the Murray Road School, some of which are quoted below, are examples of schools in this category.

3. Community

Here, community and education are synonymous. People live and learn together. Their lives, say these respondents, are fairly integrated: the emphasis in these places is on informality, intuition and "naturalness"—on people who share many levels of their lives and are building their schools together out of these lives. For example, the Claremont New School (Claremont, CA) is a day school where members have achieved a sense of community by:

> Eating and cooking together.
> Field trips (Mexico, the most extensive), skiing, camping.
> Celebrating: lots of parties, singing, etc.
> Building and creating together: our own school, the farm, etc.

It's a difficult process. Most people learn soon how to confront their own boredom.

Few of the public schools that responded to my questionnaire are striving for community in the way that Newman and Oliver define it. Some schools do not even seem to comprehend the idea while others have just begun to develop ways of making a community together:

> We have a very active PTA. Parents have been involved on various committees. We have a Lay Advisory committee from the community-at-large. We have activities such as two-day drug abuse workshops which involved students, teachers and parents with some sensitivity-type training.
> —Concord High School, Wilmington, DL.

> Cooperation with civic organizations; parental conferences; student conferences.
> —Union High School, Patagonia, AZ.

> Many phone calls, parents memos—our building is used by 33 groups weekly, from church groups to bridge clubs—a community school concept.
> —Walnut Hills Community Elementary School, Englewood, CO.

> These things are very difficult to come by in a fairly large institution. The lines of communication and channels for dialogue are kept open and sharing of decision-making is encouraged by the administration. Teachers are responsible for the development of their own curriculum and selection of their curriculum materials. Students have a great deal of choice in selecting elective courses.
> —Garfield High School, Seattle, WA

Twenty-three public schools had similar responses. This was not unexpected given the history and structure of most public schools, the emphasis on getting the material in the curriculum "covered" at the expense of everything else, the traditional expectation of how a public school should operate, the giving of grades and the ranking of students, the 9:00 to 3:00 schedules, the large size of most schools and the lack of emphasis on anything but academics and sports. Many of these schools tend to separate people by assigning narrow roles to administrators, teachers, students and parents.

These schools tend to operate as centers rather than bases and thus separate themselves from their communities. Schools then tend to mock reality: education becomes unworldly and the world becomes non-educational. Students go to school to do the teachers' work and not to do anything connected directly to their own lives or of making sense of themselves and their worlds. These practices may lead to "maximum plant efficiency," as one principal put it, but other effects are the separation of people from themselves and from others. For example, most of these schools draw 25 students (who are all about the same age) together in one room, sit them in assigned seats (often bolted to the floor) and force them not to talk or interact with each other—good training for indifference and the opposite of community.

Most of the alternative public schools which responded to my questionnaire are aware of the need for people to belong, to share and to form the school together. They say that they are striving to build community in various ways, though some have just begun to take steps in that direction. The following are typical responses by schools in this category:

> We have attempted this through the use of small tutorial groups and weekly Town Meetings; both of these devices have encountered severe difficulties and rarely function well, thus far. They are about to be modified.
> A Food Fiesta for parents, also attended by a number of students, was highly successful and provided the occasion for a friendly get-together.
> Representatives of business and cultural organizations have been invited to attend our faculty meetings.

In a thoroughly unplanned way, many students have formed interest groups. Two of these have become formally organized.

The faculty members meet weekly for a two-to-three hour session with a community psychologist to work out emotional and other problems which may hamper or disturb our working together.

Student teachers are invited to participate. These sessions and business meetings often continue to coffee, dinner and/or drinks.
—The Clinton Program, New York City

Staff responses to this would vary enormously, depending on individuals' personal assessment of where we stand now. I tend to feel that such efforts as we have made (all sorts of rituals, summer programs, after-school and weekend activities, school government efforts, Home Groups, etc., etc.) have all foundered on the rock of gross cultural differences which students in an urban polyglot group bring into the building with them. We just haven't been able to touch people very deeply—partly the result of many years of kid-assumptions that school can't touch me, shouldn't, etc. Partly the result of fantastic adult naiveté about what kids want out of school (i.e., some don't want to share, communicate, etc.—they wanna job and to get out). Building trust among fantastically hostile and uncommunicative sub-groups of students is a long, hard task, and our efforts have only scratched a surface. Retreats, meetings, calling off school to go into difficult matters, being with kids in natural hangouts, visiting in homes, etc., etc.—we could list a lot of things which we have been trying to join the

kids with the school and to each other. But ... it's bigger than us.
—Pilot Public School, Cambridge, MA

These programs involve schools with fairly small enrollments and this seems to be an important factor because community is "very difficult to come by in a fairly large institution."

Most of the private schools that responded to my questionnaire are aware of the need for community and have moved fairly far toward establishing it. These schools listed hundreds of activities that involve sharing and cooperation—singing, dancing, community meals, weekend training sessions in shared decision-making, teachers working together to develop curriculum, long community meetings using consensus to work on difficult problems, going on trips together and the like. The activities are many and varied because they grow out of unique individuals and groups who are trying to create community in schools. I could cite many schools—from ones in this study and ones that I know personally—to "prove" this, but the following should suffice:

> romantic concepts in the philosophical tradition
> the teacher dropouts along with several students live together in an old frame house—we combine almost everything. this brings many economic blessings
> in varying degrees for all involved this is emotionally very tough, very
> we all have scars and wounds that need patching; it is hard to do it sometimes
> trusting yourself, others and reality is a habit; we are working on the habit
> we patch it as we can
> don't know if we can bring it full round: "the

imperfect is our paradise," says Wallace Stevens.
—The Claremont New School, Claremont, CA

Families get together frequently. Parents work at the school with kids and teachers. Parents work together on the school. Festivals of sharing food, drink and friendship among all—parents, kids, teachers. Teachers eat often at parents' homes. Kids stay all night—or for a couple of days—at other kids' homes. Parent meetings each Thursday evening involve problem sharing, role playing, business, pleasure, food. We are separate on so many things, together on so many, growing toward community. War, racism, money, relationships, change, are continuing problems for understanding parents, kids, and teachers. We are all growing, learning, changing—toward community.
—Pepper Canyon School, La Jolla, CA

We try to create an atmosphere where openness and honesty and warmth predominate. We try to keep the decision-making process collective. The staff and volunteers understand that learning is not a one-way street, that sharing is most important and love is a meaningful word. The students respond in kind.
—People's School, Chicago, IL

By giving all we can as individuals to each other mostly: relying on individual feelings of personal responsibility. There is a natural community which forms around the goal of providing a good alternative to the established educational system, and perhaps this form provides more impetus for a sense of belonging and sharing than any other single factor. Community, I believe, has more difficulty arising if it is treated as a goal in itself than as the by-product of people working

together on the accomplishment of some more concrete objectives.
—Shasta School, San Rafael, CA

Wow. Physically, mostly. But equally, through sensitivity to personal and cultural differences. Here we feel love and are free to express love by hugging, mauling, even, sometimes biting and slugging.
We have many, many council meetings. We are so supportive you wouldn't believe it. We hassle and shout and eat and enjoy! We find kids need to find out that adults care, and care deeply, like no sleep, maybe, or get together outside of school—and that they need to find out that what they do effects community, sometimes in crucial ways. Like we can be closed down if kids act bad with outsiders or break windows in the area, etc. We act as intermediaries with parents, supporting their supportiveness, but coming down hard on their violence. It ain't easy. I've come to think Neill's job is cushy in comparison. Mainly—everybody here is here because he wants to be! That's half the battle...

Freedom includes the freedom *not to engage*! But mostly, we do. Our violence-prone kids keep involving us in dangerous activities which could bring us down, so we use this fact to reinforce community sensitivity. It takes time!
—The Free School, Albany, NY

Repeatedly, the responses from private schools are filled with similar enthusiasms, concerns and insights.

These private schools vary greatly in size, length of existence, philosophy, students' backgrounds and the like. Many were established specifically for the purpose of trying to achieve shared understanding and indicate this by putting "community" in their names.

The alternative schools quoted above do not have a monopoly on this goal. All but two of the 125 private schools in this study and a number of the public alternatives said they are striving for community. Many of the other respondents noted that they were aware of the need for developing a sense of people creating the school together. They know that community can be developed, can be learned. They also know *that developing a community is the basis for developing high academic achievement.* They may not all have achieved a high degree of community, but most are aware that "we all have scars and wounds that need patching... and that it is hard to do it sometimes... we patch it as we can."

Notes
1. "Education and Community," *Harvard Education Review*. Winter, 1967, pp. 61-106

Conclusions: Backward and Forward

What are some of the lessons to be learned from the alternative and innovative schools of the 1960s and 1970s?

The first take-away concerns the most basic question in education: *How does a child learn?* This is *the* essential question in education and seeking its answer is *the* essential quest in education. The plain and simple answer to the question is: *We do not know how a child learns.*

After all of the hundreds of years of students in classrooms, of teachers closely observing children, of thousands upon thousands of papers and books by researchers, of countless experiments by people like Piaget, of recent brain scans, minute slicing of brain tissue and MRI's, we are barely out of the alchemical age in understanding how children learn.

We have clues, insights, educated guesses, philosophies and theories, but we really do not know what goes on inside a child when she "knows," for example, that the objects in front of her, when counted, add up to four and will always add up to four.

Teachers cannot wait for the answer to the question, though, because they have 23 or so children each day who need to learn math, reading, literature, science, history and the like. Teachers need to act—act on the best evidence they have available about how children learn, how a specific child learns a specific thing, how each child learns specific things.

From where does this "evidence" come? It usually comes from years and years of practice by teachers, from teachers sharing insights with each other, from researchers and writers, from university professors passing on accumulated knowledge and it comes from psychologists, special education teachers, curriculum specialists, fiction writers, supervisors, parents and, of course, the children themselves.

Because this evidence is so vast, disconnected and, sometimes, contradictory, what teachers learn most often is selective evidence, usually information that a majority more or less agree with, what is often referred to as "traditional." Actually, the process is much more complicated than this. For example, what are the effects of state boards of education which approve textbooks? Of publishers themselves? Of federal and state departments of education? Of departments of education in universities? Of mandates from school systems?

The No Child Left Behind Act (NCLB)—along with recent efforts by various state departments of education and the National Governors' Council—have tried to codify what they deem the best of that "scientific" evidence and to require that this "common core" of knowledge and set of "best practices" be learned and used by all public school teachers.

I've noted that the accumulated evidence about learning (and teaching) is vast and, sometimes, contradictory. This has led to a great variety of beliefs, theories, practices and philosophies of education, many espoused with great passion and dedication. For example, there are those who would teach only the "basics" in math and those who will teach only the "new math," those who believe in a "discovery" approach and those who believe in rote learning or learning certain information in a prescribed way, those who follow the ideas of the Constructivists and those who adhere to E. D. Hirsch's Core Knowledge concepts.

What children learn and the depth of that learning vary widely throughout America. Why? There are multiple reasons, which include: what each teachers brings to the classroom in terms of training, knowledge, experience, skills, passion, beliefs and the like; the support teachers get; what each child brings to the classroom; what materials the teacher has available; and what approaches, methods and practices teachers employ.

Over the years, researchers have tried to figure out if children learn more effectively from a particular approach, if one approach is more effective than others. For example, the Eight-Year Study is considered by many as the best and most important educational experiment in American history. It was initiated in 1932 by the Progressive Education Association under the direction of Wilford Aikin. The study had two major goals: 1) to establish a relationship between schools and colleges that would permit and encourage the reconstruction of secondary schools and 2) to find, through exploration and experimentation, how high schools could serve youth more effectively.

The roughly 30 schools and school systems which participated differed dramatically—from elite private schools whose faculties had little interest in innovation, to large public systems like Tulsa and Denver whose faculties were eager to reconsider traditional curriculum assumptions, to university lab schools, to progressive schools throughout the country and to other quite traditional schools whose faculties had little interest in experimenting with their curriculum.

The 250 colleges that participated agreed to suspend their regular admissions criteria in favor of alternative forms of documentation provided by the schools involved.

About 1,470 students from these schools were followed for 4 years of high school and four years of college. Each of the 1,470 students was matched with a student from a non-participating school who were followed in the same manner.

Schools tried a range of approaches to teaching and learning that included traditional methods, teacher/pupil planning of learning, experiential learning, collaborative study, projects, integrated subject matter and tying academic content to student concerns and interests.

The study and its results were published in five volumes. Additional, related studies and research were published in 11 more volumes. Also, Aikin wrote a book explaining and summarizing the study.

What were the results of this extensive experiment? Students from these 30 schools achieved higher grades on exams, both at the high school and college levels, than their traditional peers. Gains were not large, but significantly, *students from the most experimental schools achieved the highest of all*. On every measure, whether academic, social or personal, students from these progressive programs were clearly more successful in college. Years later, several books were written about some of the students' experiences after college and the students from the more experimental schools were found to have full and satisfying lives.

The study was published in 1942 in the middle of WWII, so it did not attract much attention and was not widely known then, nor is it now. There has been a recent revival of interest in the Eight-Year Study, including a number of articles and books written about it.

There have been similar, though not as in-depth and grand, studies since then, including those by Ron Edmonds who examined "effective schools" in the 1980s and 1990s and a more recent, limited one, *Inside the Black Box of High-Performing, High-Poverty Schools* by Patricia J. Kannapel and Steven K. Clements. What are the results of these studies? Again, students from the more progressive, innovative schools outperformed their peers in traditional schools.

So, given the above information, why are there so few progressive schools in America today, especially since progressive education comes closest to growing out of and supporting democracy? Some researchers say that teaching in a progressive school is very difficult and not many want to undertake it; some say that parents who attended traditional schools themselves won't easily sign their kids up for a different kind of school; some attribute the lack to how education is under the influence of politics, run by remote bureaucrats in state capitals and Washington with their no children left behind and races to the top; while still others say that it is very difficult to break away from tradition, to change the way things have been done for so many years. Grace Rotzel, in *The School in Rose Valley*, writes that "any deviation from tradition is seen by some people as a threat."

I think all of these explanations are true and help explain the dearth of progressive education today. I would, though, like to examine the idea of the persistence of tradition. The best way for me to do this is by looking at the recent Catholic Church to see how what happened to it can be used as a metaphor to understand the role of tradition in education.

The Catholic Church had been going along for many decades, even centuries, in a static, insular manner. Then, in 1959, Pope John XXIII convened Vatican II, with the purpose of having the Church re-examine itself. Over several years, 2,000 religious leaders and thousands of others hammered out changes, including the following: Truth, the council said, existed outside as well as inside the Church, so Catholics were encouraged to engage with other Christian and non-Christian faiths; mass could now be said in the people's languages and not just Latin; Catholics were encouraged to grapple with the forces of the modern world, to go into prisons, deal with civil rights and poverty, be concerned with oppression and social justice. These are but a few of the changes that were wrought by Vatican II.

A new spirit arose within the Church, a positive, vital feeling, a sense of engagement and movement, a sense of rebirth.

Pope John XXIII died in 1963. The reforms he helped to bring about died not long after.

The next two popes were conservatives. They cracked down on the "liberation philosophy" that Vatican II inspired, opposed birth control and abortion, pulled back various groups that had been involved with poverty work and women's rights, cut off much of the dialogue with other religions and walled itself back up in Rome. Some clergy and parishioners resisted this return to conservatism and tradition, but the leaders of the Church co-opted some, suppressed others and isolated these dissenters and, eventually, wore them down.

Progressive education flourished from about 1900 to the late 1930s and into the 1940s. Though Progressivism dominates many educators' thinking about schooling in the first half of the 20th century, the number of schools actually using progressive methods was relatively small, limited mostly to private schools and some urban public school districts. Most public schools were unaffected by the movement, continuing to teach in conventional ways, with teachers in "telling" roles and the students seated in rows of bolted down chairs as passive recipients of the information dispensed by teachers and textbooks. When educators did adopt some practices from the progressives, they were often watered down or perverted. For example, the idea of students having concrete learning experiences became Home Economics for females and Industrial Arts for males. The same kind of perversion happened in the '60s and '70s.

Schooling in America was dramatically affected by the Great Depression and by World War II. During the Depression, most families could not pay taxes, so schools had few if any supplies; students dropped out because their families could not afford books, could not afford to clothe them or the children were needed to help support the family; schools often could not pay teachers or could only pay very low wages; and many schools were forced to close. It was a crisis time when people pulled back into the "tried and true." So, if a teacher or a school wanted to experiment with progressive ideas, they were quickly shot down by parents and administrators.

Of course, schooling during WWII was not a primary or even a secondary concern given that the entire country was focused on the war.

After the war, with an explosion of children and more families moving into the middle class, public schooling came to the forefront. It was a time when a number of crucial events occurred that set the foundation for today's education: small schools (especially one-room ones) were replaced with larger, non-local schools and small districts were merged into larger ones. The larger schools and districts along with state departments of education became bureaucratized and standardized, establishing more central controls on schools—from textbooks and materials, to teacher training, curriculum requirements, hours of attendance and the like. The efforts reached a kind of peak in the 1950s when "teacher-proof" curricula were put into place in many school districts.

The idea behind teacher-proofing the curriculum was to minimize teachers' control of curriculum development, with all of its unevenness and lack of "quality control," by creating a seemingly firm bond among educational objectives, curriculum content and assessment tools. Teachers, then, would not be able to stand in the way between the student and the supposedly rich curriculum materials. These materials were developed by specialized curriculum experts—not in the schools, but in publishing houses, colleges and state departments of education—to be used in a cookbook fashion so that any teachers using the materials would have the same results.

This view of teaching and learning assumes that there is a "right way" to teach, a content relevant to all and curricula which can be developed in a certain way so that all children can learn it in the same way.

Another view of the teaching-learning process holds

that it is only the teacher who knows her students' learning needs well enough to continuously modify the classroom and the curriculum in response to these needs. Therefore, this view holds, it is the teacher who must develop her/his own curriculum. Between these poles, there are other views. There are those who understand the importance of high-quality curriculum materials and who also understand the important role of the teacher in relationship to how s/he uses these materials. Progressive educators add one more ingredient to this view: *the child and how that child learns and how the teacher mediates between the child and the curriculum*, which, as John Dewey explained, is a continuum.

In the 1960s and into the '70s, there was a broad cultural reaction to the conservatism of the 1950s, often characterized as "the greening of America." Of course, this reaction happened in education and is the subject of this book.

The period prior to the '60s was a conservative time: teachers talked at the children who were expected to sit quietly in their bolted-down desks; teachers taught cover-to-cover from textbooks, which were remarkably similar throughout the country; parents had little or no influence over what went on inside the school buildings; schools separated themselves from the "world out there"; teachers taught, administrators administered and parents parented.

I think we are coming to the end of another long period of educational conservatism, a time of reaction to the '60s and '70s, a reaction similar to the one in the Catholic Church after Pope John XXIII. The Bush No Child Left Behind Act and the Obama Race To The Top centralized control of schooling at the federal and state levels in remote bureaucracies, steamrolling just about every innovation that had arisen during the previous thirty years.

This means that the time is ripe again for questioning: time to ask if having state-mandated standards and curricula is the best way to provide for children's learning; to question the high stakes testing at practically every grade level with the big club of no diploma if the tests are not passed; schools sanctioned, and put on "watch" or into "corrective action." It's time to question everything wrought by NCLB, RTTT and, now, Common Core.

As noted in the Introduction, innovative and alternative school people in the '60s and '70s did such questioning. Out of this questioning, they developed many different kinds of schools—many new and effective ways to teach and learn, as I've shown throughout this book.

So, this period could serve as a kind of "model" for today's educators, a model that could help them to change what's happening in schools, but not to necessarily create the same kinds of schools that existed then, though this would not be a bad thing. One main idea is to learn from and to emulate the questioning and the questing that occurred then.

There are a number of other ideas, both large and small, which we can take away from that time. One major lesson is that learning is personal. We, each of us, are learners. That's what humans do: we learn in our own ways and in our own time; we take in the most, though, when that which is to be learned means something to us, is connected to us and is encountered in an active, involved way. This idea runs through each and every chapter in this book, from the initial two very personal stories about my children, to how children are taught in Margaret Skutch's Early Learning Center, to "One of You Is Sufficient" and "Strawberry Fields Forever," culminating in the last chapter on community. Indeed, learning is personal but not in a selfish sense because learning almost always occurs in some type of larger social setting, just as we as individuals can only live and thrive in larger social settings.

The necessary, logical corollary to the idea that learning is personal is the idea that school then must be personal. If that's the way kids learn best, then that's the way they need to be taught, the way schools need to structure themselves. There is no choice but to make sure that each and every child is cared for, is provided for, in each and every school.

How, then, are children to be taught? The answer is also in each chapter in this book. *Children learn from experience*, as John Dewey and others have shown over the years, and they learn best when *actively* involved in their own learning. This is done with hands-on materials and with learning projects orchestrated by a skillful teacher extending and deepening a child's interests.

Let me illustrate: Mary DiSchino was a grades 3-4 teacher at the Graham & Parks Alternative Public School (Cambridge, MA). Mary was not pleased with the way science was learned in her class, so she decided to ask the children what they were interested in.

Mary did a brain-storming session with the kids who listed all kinds of things they were curious about and Mary put each one up on the board as the children spoke: dinosaurs, how TV works, earwax, taking apart appliances to see how they work, how birds lay eggs, how plants grow, etc. By the end of the session the children had come up with about 35 items.

Then the children voted on what they'd like to learn about first. They choose ear wax. (I witnessed this session and said to myself, "Ear wax?")

So, Mary set about developing lessons on ear wax. We had several doctors as parents in the school and from them she got models of the skull, take-apart models of the ear, books on the ear and the like. It was also fortuitous that Mary had been on the *Andrea Dora* when it sank and her ears were damaged so she had to wear hearing aids as a result of the accident.

Over the next few weeks, the children explored the structure of the ear, messing with the models, learning how the ear works, why there is ear wax, how it's formed, how hearing can go bad, etc.—reading about it, examining the models, taking them apart, having a hearing test and talking with one of the parent doctors.

At the end of this "ear wax" learning unit, the students did an exhibition of what they had learned, showing off their research papers, the models they had used or made, the books they had read, etc. to their parents and the rest of the students and staff in our school, one class at a time.

The children then went on to study about the various parts of the body in depth, being especially fascinated with bones and how they fit and worked together, in humans and in animals (especially birds).

The world's a wonderous place. When young children explore their curiosities in this way, worlds then open up to them—the worlds of math, art, sciences, music, reading and on and on. Their need to know often leads to profound discoveries.

There need not be one set curriculum, whether developed by the school, the district or the state. There is way too much of importance to know in this world to be able to stuff it into a set curriculum. Teachers, children and schools need to be given the right and the responsibility to decide what to teach and to learn. In this way, schools will not only be able to meet the individual needs of the children, but they will be excited about the subject matter the children learn. They will be vested in it and will work hard for each child to learn it. It's been my experience that when teachers are empowered in this way they will do extraordinary things.

Of course, there are some "basics" that schools must teach—how to read, how to do math, to write, to know history and the like, all at high levels. Schools must teach these basics, equip kids with the tools and the knowledge to be on-going learners. *How* these are taught is the important thing. There is a vast gulf between learning them by having a teacher talk at you, reading them in a textbook, memorizing them and being tested to having a student actively involved with hands-on learning materials and with doing learning projects that come out of the children's interests. A child can learn much about how to ice skate from a manual, but she will not really learn how until she straps on a pair of skates and goes out onto the ice. She will get better at skating if someone can help her look at what she is doing and find ways to improve upon it.

But schools which teach only basics will not truly succeed because they must also teach skills, concepts and ideas. This is what the good alternative and innovative schools did very well. Also, they often wrapped the basics, the skills, the concepts and the ideas into a unified whole through extended, integrated learning projects that involved hands-on materials, books, films, computers, writing, discussions, music, uses of primary materials, art, learning in the community and the like to explore issues in depth. *The child is guided to understand and extend the learning embedded in his/her experiences.* The adults—sensitive, positive, skilled, experienced—are the ones who must carefully guide and extend the child's learning.

As noted earlier, good schools empower their teachers to develop their own curriculum, which does not mean rejecting commercially produced materials. Teachers develop curricula using a variety of sources: groups such as the National Council of Teachers of Mathematics, state departments of education, consultants, books and journals, private companies like TERC, school district specialists, and the like. These schools also develop a variety of structures to help their teachers to work collaboratively, sharing what they know, teaching each other, learning from each other, spurring each other on to get better and better.

Schools where this happens develop high standards for their faculty and for their children. The alternative and innovative schools developed high standards without resorting to standardization.

Initially, where did these new schools in the '60s and '70s get the kind of people needed to teach in student-centered ways? Most of the teachers had been traditional ones who had begun to question what they had been doing and began to try new ideas, different methods and materials. For example, some began to use experiments as the basis for teaching science, or whole language combined with phonics to teach reading or to use a variety of manipulatives and projects to teach math. Most of these kept on learning, expanding and deepening their craft.

Some learned in these new schools, in ways similar to what Margaret Skutch established in her school. Someone— the director, a master teacher, a consultant, faculty from a university—would lead regular workshop sessions in the school for new (and, often, "old") teachers, helping them to acquire skills, ideas, methods and materials. Teachers visited each other's classrooms and teachers held sessions to show colleagues what s/he was doing.

In my school in Cambridge, we had a full-time staff developer who supported new teachers in their classrooms, spread new ideas throughout the school, helped find materials, ran workshops, spearheaded curriculum changes and the like. For a number of years, we hired full-time Instructional Aides in each classroom. These usually were people who aspired to be teachers—some were in a teacher training program already or had a degree in another field and wanted to become certified. They worked for a number of years, gradually learning from the teacher as an apprentice would, taking on more and more responsibility as they gained experience. We then hired them as teachers or they were hired by other student-centered schools.

Of course, there were colleges and universities that became centers of educational change. Lillian Webber and other faculty at New York University were early leaders in developing programs and courses that taught teachers more student-centered approaches. The Center for Teaching and Learning at the University of North Dakota, under the leadership of Vito Perrone, was also a leader in this area, providing such programs for undergraduate and graduate students. (Vito also founded the North Dakota Study Group on Evaluation that helped schools develop a large variety of alternative assessments and accountability measures.)

The Boston area was rich with university help for area schools: Lesley, Wheelock, Tufts and Simmons developed programs to helped prepare teachers for open classrooms. Some faculty specialized in the "new" math, the uses of manipulatives (multi-base blocks, geo boards, etc.) and projects to not only teach facts and skills but also concepts; some, like Brenda Engels, focused on alternative forms of evaluation; some focused on science or reading or social studies or on how to develop an integrated curriculum.

Another, important lesson from this period is that schools exist in and of the world. As such, they need to bring that world into the school and they need to take their children out to meet that world. This, also, means that schools have to actively engage kids with issues like social and economic justice, racism, the social class structure of society and the like, as is the case in "One of You is Sufficient."

There are additional ideas to be carried away from the '60s and '70s. For example, size matters. How small or large should a school be? Various researchers and practitioners from that time explored this issue and came to recommend that schools have anywhere from 60 or so students up to about 250.

The important issue concerning size is personalization. Good schools depend on close contacts among people. When a school gets too big, it loses the ability to really know well each student, staff and parent. Then, it begins to bureaucratize. When it is too small, there are not enough relationships and interactions for learning.

When I was principal of the Graham & Parks Alternative Public School, I was able to experience the school as small since it started as a K-4 school that we grew to K-8 with about 210 children. We then almost doubled it by merging with another school. I felt we were able to maintain close, personal contacts with up to about 350 kids. After that, we could see those contacts diminishing in quantity and in quality.

Is one grade arrangement better than others in how schools are structured? Should we have K-4 or K-6 schools, followed by middle schools and then high schools? Or is it better to have a K-8 arrangement? Evidence from the '70s indicates that a K-8 arrangement gives educators a better chance to really get to know children and their families very well and, thus, to serve them better. It was also my experience that these schools were able to develop curriculum better, doing it by "planning backwards" from the 8th grade, with all of the teachers working together in one building. There is current research to support this notion: having more transitions from K-8 tends to lower a child's achievement level. There is no better structure than K-8 to help a school develop community.

Should classes be single-graded or multi-graded? If a school is concerned with developing community, then multi-graded classrooms give teachers a better chance to do so since children from a wider range have increased opportunities to interact. But single-graded classroom can "loop." For example, a 3rd grade class and its teacher can stay together into 4th grade, then the following year the teacher can loop back to 3rd grade when her children move on to 5th grade. The point here is clear: it is important for a school to develop various structures which help to promote community. If looping works to do this, fine; if multi-grading works, fine, too.

At the Graham & Parks, we experimented with various grade combinations in our initial ten years, having such combinations as K-l, K-1-2, 1-2, 1-2-3, 2-3, 2-3-4, Junior and Senior K's and so on. Teachers came to feel, though, that a three-grade spread was difficult to do well and so we went back to double-graded classes.

In Waldorf schools, which began to spread widely during the '60s, teachers stay with their class from kindergarten through 8th grade. In this structure, a teacher truly gets to know his/her students and parents so that personalization can be really optimized.

It is clear that NCLB dominates education today, but this does not mean that it holds the education field exclusively. There are those who believe in and practice different forms of education—forms quite similar to what existed 30-40 years ago.

There is a revival of Constructivism; new interest in the ideas of Lev Vygotsky; new writing about progressive education from Eleanor Duckworth, Ron Berger (on developing quality student work and on project-based learning), Deborah Meier, Ted Sizer, Linda Hutchinsen, Courtney Cazden and Howard Gardner, among others; a growth in the number of public and private Montessori schools; groups like Project Zero at Harvard, the Coalition of Essential Schools, the Alternative Education Resources Organization, and Expeditionary Learning which support these "different" teachers and schools; and there are a number of alternative and innovative schools from the '60s and '70s still very much alive.

Finally, I should note that newer innovative and alternative schools are also very much alive today. There are several hundred of them—mostly private—and they are spread throughout the country. One only needs to look at the Alternative Education Resource Organization's list of schools to confirm this. (See www.EducationRevolution.org). Some of the current charter schools also exemplify the best aspects of the kind of education I've presented in this book.

Even though these current efforts are relatively small, they are important for a number of reasons: they show the power of the ideas and practices from the '60s and '70s because they have been able to survive in an environment which is more than just hostile. It is important for today's educators to know this: in addition to going back to recover the educational past, teachers and administrators have current schools to visit and see these "different" practices first-hand; and they have current writers and support organizations to talk with and get help from if they decide to move ahead with adapting, adopting or developing innovative and alternative practices and institutions.

Charter schools grew out of the innovative and alternative schools of the '60s and '70s. They remain controversial, even among progressive educators. Charter schools were initially leftist in their beliefs and practices. Then, educators and politicians on the right appropriated them to further their goal of breaking up the virtual monopoly of public schools and replacing them with a market-driven plan of privatized schooling. One other thing is fairly clear about most charter schools: they are individualistic, isolated hotbeds of change for small groups of students, but they usually have little effect on other schools around them.

My experience leads me to prefer "controlled choice" plans for public schools over charter schools. Well-run choice programs usually compel schools in a district to compete for students, which causes them to innovate, to develop ways to attract parents and students. Choice programs acknowledge that children learn in different ways and that parents should have the right to place their children in schools which fit their children's needs. Also, by being a part of a school system, educators in these choice schools have many opportunities to influence each other, of spreading their successful ideas and practices among each other and of spurring each other to higher and higher levels of achievement. For example, the alternative public school that I ran in Cambridge (MA) spun off three other similar programs, changed how early childhood education was provided, how mathematics was taught, how parents were involved, along with many other effects on the entire district.

As an alternative to schooling, some parents choose to homeschool their children. Initially, in the mid-1960's, there were a few thousand children being homeschooled, but the number has now grown to around 1.77 million children, about

3.4 percent of the total K-12 school population. Most of these children are White (68%), while 15% are Hispanic, eight percent Black and four percent Asian or Pacific Islanders.

Parents choose to homeschool their children for three basic reasons: because the public schools do not meet their religious or moral needs, the public schools do not meet their children's academic needs, or the social and emotional climate of public schools is not supportive of their children. A number of parents homeschool because they think this is the best way to educate their children—in a loving, caring environment where they believe they can provide for all of their children's needs.

Over the years, a large number of support groups for homeschooling have grown up across the country, including the Alternative Education Resources Organization. Home School World (homeschool.com) lists such groups by state, with several states having a dozen or more groups, large and small.

These groups can provide curriculum materials, legal advice, moral support and more to homeschooling families. Some are centers for homeschooled children to meet for academic, social or sports reasons. There is also a vast amount of information and curricular materials available on line—from math, to science, to social studies, to the arts and even to physical education and nutrition. Now, using these many resources, it's possible for parents to develop a very sophisticated education for their children. Some even work out arrangements to have their children utilize resources in their local public schools-- from classes, to equipment, to physical education and sports. In several California districts, the homeschooled population is so large that the districts specifically provide for them.

When John Holt first began to support homeschooling, he and I had a series of discussions about it and I was opposed because the kids were mostly isolated at home. Now, with the large increase in supports, I am not opposed to kids being educated at home. But I have a major concern: Do parents understand our base-ten mathematical system, the phonetic/phonemic structure of English, a variety of sciences, and how writers structure prose and poetry for example? There is no way for us to know, but my sense is that some do and that many probably do not.

When I lived in south New Jersey, there was a local family that decided to homeschool their child. The local school district took them to court to force them back into the public schools. I got to know the family and I invited them to have their child attend my alternative school on days they wanted and then I was an expert witness for them at the trial, which they won. So, I see homeschooling as a complicated affair.

Another large idea in this book is that a great deal of learning is a social activity, an idea that John Dewey emphasized and one that was explored in a different and as profound way by Lev Vygotsky. We are social beings—we learn with and from other people, all in social and societal settings. A group can often enhance the individual. Learning in schools takes place in settings where there are children and adults mixed together with each other. So, schools need to structure themselves to facilitate children learning in social ways, whether through cooperative learning groups, pairs and the like, making sure that children are actively involved together in learning.

This idea leads us to the culminating idea in the book: that it is the school's job to develop a strong community in each classroom and in the school as a whole. Developing a high-functioning school community is the end product of the idea that learning is a social activity.

The quotation from the Shasta School in the last chapter makes *the* important point about the need for community in schools: *It is through developing a strong community that a school can achieve high academic success.*

Imbedded in community is the idea of democracy. The beginning of democracy is in a child's choosing what s/he needs to learn. It is there when the child is an essential part of what goes on in the teaching/learning process, when s/he has an important say in what happens. Democracy is then extended when those involved in a school are part of the decision-making processes of that school. This is seen in the Mary DiSchino example noted above and it is seen in a number of the quotations in the community chapter: "...[P]eople working together on the accomplishment of... concrete goals"; "[M]any, many council meetings"; and "We try to make the decision-making process collective."

Democracy is one of the important aspects of the innovative and alternative schools in the '60s and '70s. Elementary and high schools held frequent community meetings and decisions were often made by consensus. When I was principal of the Graham & Parks Alternative Public School, we devised a number of ways to involve parents and staff equally in all decision-making, whether hiring, firing, curriculum, policies or whatever. The school was run by an elected group of equal numbers of parents and staff, including me (with one vote), and all decisions were finalized by this group. My experience is that our decisions were stronger, were made better, were enhanced because of our shared decision-making processes. We were not the only ones to do this: numerous public and private schools, both large and small, successfully involved students, staff and parents in all of the decision-making.

Most Americans do not experience democracy outside of voting. Few families are run as democracies and few businesses are operated on democratic principles. There are hardly any institutions or groups where one can participate in a meaningful way in the operation of the organization. Only a relatively few people actually influence political decision-making and most of that occurs outside of the voting booth. So, it is no wonder that schools are not models of and for democracy. But that does not mean it can't be done: it was done, as I've noted, in many of the public and private student-centered schools and a fair number of democratic schools operate successfully today.

This is what many innovative and alternative schools in the '60s and '70s came to understand: When a diverse group of parents, staff and students are involved together in the daily making of a school, in all aspects of the school's functioning, when they are respected, trusted, supported and empowered, then they will individually and collectively own that school and will do everything in their power to make it a successful place for kids.

About the Author

LEN SOLO is an educational consultant who supports principals and teacher leaders. His prior work includes teaching kindergarten through the university level, establishing and chairing a teacher preparation program in a New Jersey college, serving as principal of the K-8 Graham & Parks Alternative Public School (Cambridge, MA), and serving as the interim principal of Cambridge Rindge and Latin High School.

Solo is the author of four volumes of poetry, *Making an Extraordinary School: The Work of Ordinary People* about the Graham & Parks School, and a short story collection, *The Turning of the Dark*. He continues to write poetry, short stories, and on education.

www.ingramcontent.com/pod-product-compliance
Lightning Source LLC
Chambersburg PA
CBHW031138090426
42738CB00008B/1133